THE PLAYS OF SAMUEL BECKETT

BY THE SAME AUTHOR

Samuel Beckett: A Study of his Novels

EUGENE WEBB

The Plays of
SAMUEL BECKETT

PETER OWEN

London

ISBN 0 7206 0352 8

PETER OWEN LIMITED
12 Kendrick Mews Kendrick Place London SW7

First British Commonwealth Edition 1972
© 1972 by the University of Washington Press

Printed in Great Britain by
Bristol Typesetting Co Ltd St Philips Bristol

For Teri

ACKNOWLEDGMENTS

Permission to quote from the following works by Samuel Beckett has been kindly granted by Grove Press, Inc.: *Cascando,* copyright © 1963 by Samuel Beckett; *Words and Music,* copyright © 1962 by Samuel Beckett; *Eh Joe,* copyright © 1967 by Samuel Beckett; *Play,* copyright © 1964 by Samuel Beckett; *Come and Go,* copyright © 1968 by Samuel Beckett; *Film,* copyright © 1967 by Samuel Beckett; *Endgame, Act Without Words,* copyright © 1958 by Grove Press, Inc.; *Happy Days,* copyright © 1964 by Grove Press, Inc.; *Krapp's Last Tape, All That Fall, Embers, Act Without Words II,* copyright © 1957 by Samuel Beckett, copyright © 1958, 1959, 1960 by Grove Press, Inc.; *Waiting for Godot,* copyright © 1954 by Grove Press, Inc.; *Bram Van Velde,* copyright © 1958 by Georges Fall, Paris; *Malone Dies,* copyright © 1956 by Grove Press, Inc.; *The Unnamable,* copyright © 1958 by Grove Press, Inc.; *Proust,* all rights reserved, first published 1931; *Watt,* all rights reserved, first published by The Olympia Press, Paris, 1953, first American edition 1959; *Molloy,* all rights reserved in all countries by The Olympia Press, Paris and Grove Press, New York, first Grove Press edition 1955.

Passages from the following works of Samuel Beckett are quoted by permission of Faber and Faber Ltd.: *Waiting for Godot, All That Fall, Endgame, Krapps Last Tape, Embers, Act Without Words I, Act Without Words II, Happy Days, Words and Music, Cascando, Play, Film,* and *Eh Joe.* Passages from the following works of Samuel Beckett are quoted by permission of Calder and Boyars Ltd.: *Watt, Molloy, Malone Dies, The Unnamable, Bram Van Velde, Proust,* and *Come and Go.* Random House, Inc., and Alfred A. Knopf, Inc., have kindly granted permission to quote from " The Anecdote of the Jar " by Wallace Stevens, copyrighted by Alfred A. Knopf, Inc.

CONTENTS

THE PLAYS OF SAMUEL BECKETT

CHAPTER I

Introduction: Beckett and the Philosophical Tradition of the Absurd

> . . . suffering finds no vent in action
> . . . a continuous state of mental distress is prolonged, unrelieved by incident, hope, or resistance . . . there is everything to be endured, nothing to be done. In such situations there is inevitably something morbid, in the description of them something mono-tonous. When they occur in actual life, they are painful, not tragic; the representation of them in poetry is painful also.

An early, faintly hostile review of *Waiting for Godot*? Perhaps the word "poetry" is a giveaway, though *Godot* brought to the theater of the early 1950's a more poetic language than was usually heard in plays of this century. No, the writer in this case is Matthew Arnold, and the subject is his own poem on the suicide of Empe-docles — a Victorian poet describing the mental anguish of a Greek philosopher of the fifth century B.C.[1] The passage can serve nevertheless as a surprisingly appropriate critique of what has re-cently come to be called the literature of the absurd. It describes with great precision the state of mind this literature portrays, while at the same time it reminds us that both its concern and its torment are as old as human thought.

The history of man's speculations about the universe and human life in relation to it shows a continual movement back and forth between two constantly present poles : one a vision of wholeness and meaningful pattern, a vision of cosmos, the other a vision of chaos. This movement arises from the tension between a desire on the one hand to construct mental pictures of reality which will make it intelligible, and a need on the other to criticize these, to determine whether or not the interpretive concepts so formed do in fact correspond to reality. This tension has probably been present in the mind of any man who has ever thought, and it has certainly been a feature of the intellectual life of every civilization. In a given historical period, however, one usually finds either that one of these tendencies has temporarily gained the upper hand, or that whichever of the two has been dominant is giving way before the revived force of the other.

In the western world, both the classical and, for want of a better word, the modern civilizations can be seen to have gone through alternating waves of this kind. Matthew Arnold, for example, as a nineteenth century heir to what Marjorie Nicolson has called "the breaking of the circle,"[2] felt himself living in an age in which all the traditional concepts that gave life its meaning were being threatened with chaos and anarchy. Consequently, as he looked from his position back to that of Empedocles, he felt with the Greek philosopher the kinship of those who are, in Arnold Toynbee's phrase "philosophically contemporaneous" :

> I intended to delineate the feelings of one of the last of the Greek religious philosophers...having survived his fellows, living on into a time when the habits of Greek thought and feeling had begun fast to change, character to dwindle, the influence of the Sophists to prevail. Into the feelings of a man so situated there entered much that we are accustomed to consider as exclusively modern. . . . What those who are familiar only with the great monuments of early Greek genius suppose to be its exclusive characteristics, have disappeared : the calm, the cheerfulness, the disinterested objectivity have disappeared; the dialogue of the mind with itself has commenced; modern problems have presented themselves; we hear already the doubts, we witness the discouragement, of Hamlet and of Faust.[3]

And, we might add from our own point in time, of Murphy and Molloy, of Vladimir and Clov.

Concern with the absurd, then, is a phenomenon both contemporary and historical. The word itself means irrational or incongruous, and in its earliest uses (in Latin) it referred to disharmony or dissonance. In its current use as a term to describe a literary movement, it refers to the absence of meaning, either in the sense of intelligible pattern or in the sense of value.

All men, says Aristotle, desire to know.[4] And, since men are as they are, to know means to see both pattern and purpose. When the universe does not seem to offer this kind of meaning or even to allow the possibility of it, the inevitable human response is frustration, which if prolonged becomes the sort of dull anguish so poignantly described in the opening quotation from Arnold.

This is the state of mind Samuel Beckett explores in his novels and plays. As an educated and widely read man, Beckett is well acquainted not only with the despair of modern man but also with the long history of thought that has led to it.[5] His works contain allusions to philosophical thinkers ranging from the pre-Socratics to Heidegger, Sartre, and Wittgenstein.[6] This thorough familiarity with the intellectual roots of the modern mind is one of the principal sources of Beckett's great comprehensiveness and power. For this reason it may be worthwhile to take a brief look at some of the figures who constitute the tradition upon which he draws.

Although, as we have seen, the absurd is not a problem new to our century, the problem is probably more acute now than ever before. The man of the twentieth century who looks back on the preceding three millennia that make up his cultural biography is confronted with the wreckage of a dishearteningly large number of systems of thought. These are the "corpses" to which Vladimir and Estragon refer in the second act of *Waiting for Godot*. "Thinking is not the worst," says Vladimir, "What is terrible is to have thought."[7] The spectacle of the failure of so many attempts to explain man and the universe, attempts begun with *élan* but ending either in blind alleys or with their apparent initial conquests eroded by skepticism, imposes on the modern mind a special insecurity.

The earliest attempt in western civilization at a systematic, rational explanation of reality is traditionally thought to have been that of the Milesian hylozoists in the sixth century B.C. Thales, the founder of this school, tried to do two things : to explain the nature of matter by identifying a common material principle to which all more complex substances could be theoretically reduced, and to explain the relationship between matter and spirit. To solve the first problem he chose water as the common ground of all material substance; to solve the second he developed a theory that all matter contains spirit — or at least this is what Aristotle thought Thales must have meant by the idea that "all things are full of gods."[8] As one might expect, the subsequent thinkers in this school refined the thought of Thales to the point of radical uncertainty. Anaximander, not satisfied with water as the common ground of matter, chose something far less concrete and intelligible which he called the Boundless or Unlimited. Already apophasis, the mode of discourse appropriate to the irreducibly mysterious, was making its entry. Heraclitus of Ephesus, the last of this school, carried the hylozoist approach to its logical end.

In the thought of Heraclitus, the emphasis is on the constancy of change, the material principle of which, he believed, could only be fire. "Everything flows and nothing abides," he says, "everything gives way and nothing stays fixed."[9] Everything is in a state of becoming; nothing ever *is* : "You cannot step twice into the same river, for other waters and yet others go ever flowing on."[10] Being is not intelligible to man, because it can never be extracted from the flux of time. Although Heraclitus had no intention of denying all coherent order (he assumed that the constant change took place according to a universal Logos, or rational principle), the implication of his thought is that the order that exists is almost entirely beyond man's apprehension. And since man's reason has no material in immediate experience upon which it can operate, man can hardly be said to be rational : "Man is not rational; there is intelligence only in what encompasses him."[11] Consequently, although there may be a "hidden harmony,"[12] it can be of little use to man. The universe of human experience "is but a heap of rubbish piled up at random."[13] Thus the effort begun by Thales ended in something very like a vision of the absurd.

The attempt in Elea by Parmenides and his disciple, Zeno, to rescue being from this flux and to re-establish the supremacy of reason led in turn into its own special cul-de-sac. Parmenides taught that being is one and unchanging, and that if there appears to be change, then the appearance is false. If the senses speak of becoming, then the senses lie. Zeno (probably the "old Greek" to whom Clov refers in *Endgame*[14]) used the weapon of his paradoxes to support this position. The logical consequence of this approach, however, is that while being in the abstract is intelligible, experience is not. The arrow never moves; Achilles will never pass his tortoise. The triumph of pure reason is a Pyrrhic victory at best : reason rules supreme, but isolated in the mind.

It was in an attempt to use the doctrine of a plurality of

interacting elements as a means of threading his way between the rock of Being and the whirlpool of Becoming that Empedocles was driven into what Arnold called "the dialogue of the mind with itself." Empedocles chose four elements as the building blocks of his universe — air, earth, fire, and water — but the movement he began in such relative simplicity ended with the innumerable atoms of Leucippus and Democritus. Empedocles could still believe that objective reality was not too remote from human experience, but Democritus divided knowledge into two types, the "obscure," derived from the senses, and the "genuine," that of the intellect working abstractly : "By convention there is sweet, by convention there is bitter, by convention hot and cold, by convention color; but in reality there are only atoms and the void." Democritus himself recognized the danger implicit in this schism between human experience and a "truth" that "lies in the abyss" : "Do not try to understand everything," he warned his disciples, "lest you thereby be ignorant of everything." Looking back upon the history of speculative philosophy since his time, we can see how prophetic were the words spoken by "Senses" in his dialogue between the intellect and the senses : "Ah wretched intellect, you get your evidence only as we give it to you, and yet you try to overthrow us. That overthrow will be your downfall."[15]

Another movement, which took quite a different approach from that just described, was Pythagoreanism, a school of thought in which Beckett's Murphy was interested at one stage of his career.[16] The Pythagoreans had certain advantages over those who tried to explain reality by way of an analysis of matter. Since they were interested primarily in numerical relationships, that is, in abstract patterns, they did not have to concern themselves with the intricacies of matter. Pythagoras is supposed to have come upon number as the key to understanding when he discovered the octave and some other harmonic relationships in music. From that base, he is said to have gone on to the discovery of the Pythagorean theorem in geometry and from there to astronomy, through which he discovered the "music of the spheres," a set of numerical relationships among the planets. Experienced reality, from this point of view, became a union of the abstract and concrete, with the focus on its more tractable abstract side. This doctrine provided for its followers satisfying cognitive patterns, and purpose as well : the perception and contemplation of harmony could, they believed, purify the soul and thus prepare it for spiritual advancement in future incarnations.

The difficulty they ran into in their system, however, was that, having put all of their eggs in the abstract basket, they discovered it had a hole in it: the mystery of incommensurables. The Pythagorean theorem worked beautifully for a right triangle with sides and hypotenuse in the ratio 3:4:5. The sum of the squares of the smaller sides adds up to the square of the hypotenuse, and the progressive ratios of the three sides are neatly patterned. With an isoceles triangle on the other hand, they found not only that the hypotenuse did not have so tidy a ratio to the smaller sides, but also that it could not even be calculated. The square root of two (the smaller sides are in a 1:1 ratio, so that the formula for the hypotenuse is $\sqrt{1^2 + 1^2}$) is a number which can never be finally resolved. Like the number of weeks in the year divided into the number of days, a problem that seems to have weighed on Beckett's Watt, it can be calculated to infinity.[17] The Pythagoreans tried to keep this information secret, but did not succeed. In Beckett's *Murphy* we are told the fate of the "babbler," Hippasos: " 'Drowned in a puddle,' said Neary, 'for having divulged the incommensurability of side and diagonal.' "[18]

Confronted with the complexities and logical impasses of all of these various attempts to determine what reality in fact is, apart from the mind that perceives it, the Sophists, represented for example by Protagoras, decided that objective external reality was less important than its subjective appearance to man. "Matter," said Protagoras, "is essentially the sum of all the seemings that it has for any and all persons."[19] This was a way out of the puzzle, and it has proven a very durable principle of inquiry. In fact it still has a following today, in an oblique way, in logical empiricism, pragmatism, and phenomenology. This approach to knowledge has never had wide appeal, however; if "all men desire to know," most men want to be able to believe that what they know has a concrete relation to another reality outside the mind.

The attempt to bring together the elements of experience, both mental and physical, into a unified picture was carried further by Plato and his pupil, Aristotle. Plato founded his epistemological certainty on the theory of an immediate intellectual intuition of essences. For Plato, concrete things were composed of form (the essence, or supersensible organizing principle, of the thing) and matter, Form, he thought, was more real than matter; it could even have an objective reality apart from the material things in which it was embodied. Perfect forms, according to Plato, had real existence on a higher plane of being, while concrete material things were more or less inadequate imitations of them. This approach to the understanding of reality made knowledge objective, but it raised in a new and disturbing way the problem of the relationship between spirit and matter. Thales had regarded spirit as simply the inner life of matter, but the association of the form of the thing with an independent realm of spirit, which moreover was thought to be more real than that of matter, had the effect of splitting concrete being in two. The subsequent development of this mode of thought proceeded in two quite different directions. One was that of the neo-Platonists, the best known of whom was Plotinus. This school attempted to solve the problem by focusing on spirit as the primary reality and reducing matter virtually to nonbeing or illusion. The other approach was that of Aristotle.

Aristotle attempted to hold concrete reality together. He accepted Plato's theory of the intellectual intuition of form, but believed that form could exist only in its concrete embodiment in a particular being. Form and matter were organically united; neither could exist without the other. To explain how a man can have an immediate intuition of a form embodied in a concrete thing, he assumed that there must be a special mental faculty, the "Active Intellect," which was able to reach outside the body and become, spiritually, the form it intuited. The advantage of this epistemology was that it unified the elements of being and put man in immediate touch with genuinely objective reality. The fragility of such a theory, however, should be obvious. The whole theory is based on a set of assumptions that cannot possibly be verified by any method, either rational or empirical. Its principal claim to assent was the emotional appeal it had for men who wanted to believe in the unified vision it offered. This is no small claim for the heart, as the Aristotelian revival in the Middle Ages showed, but the questioning intellect is more difficult to satisfy. The monument that Aristotle constructed was chipped away at over a period of centuries by skeptics from Pyrrho to Sextus Empiricus. It was not until sixteen hundred years after his death that Aristotle won the allegiance of a large part of the western world.

Modern civilization has seen the rebirth, in various forms, of all these systems of thought. The philosophical speculations of the early

Middle Ages were mainly Platonist in orientation. The emphasis that this tradition placed on the spiritual side of reality probably made it seem especially suitable for adaptation to a Christian frame of reference, particularly since during much of this period the material side of life must have seemed extremely intractable. In the high Middle Ages, however, western man began to recover confidence in his ability to manage the temporal world, and consequently became interested once again in wrestling with matter. The rediscovery of Aristotle at about this time provided intellectual tools with which to begin again the attempt to explain the relation between spirit and matter and to analyze the structure of physical reality. It is probably significant that the person most responsible for the revival of interest in Aristotle in the European Middle Ages was not only a theologian but also one of the period's most important scientists : Albertus Magnus.

It was Thomas Aquinas, a pupil of Albertus, who completed the work of adapting Aristotle to a Christian frame of reference. The result was a unified vision of man, body and soul organically united, at home in the flesh and on the earth. The larger universe was a divinely ordered cosmos centered upon man, the proper heir to creation. This vision received poetic formulation in the *Divine Comedy* of Dante, a writer in whom Beckett has been interested since his university days and who has been a major influence on his work.[20]

The synthesis did not hold together long, however. Not long after Dante had finished transmuting its vision into *terza rima,* other thinkers, especially William of Ockham and Nicholas of Autrecourt, began to undermine its foundations. Ockham and Autrecourt challenged the most basic assumptions of Aristotelian epistemology : the reality of forms as objects of intellectual intuition, the reliability of the senses, and even the principle of causality. When René Descartes's method of systematic doubt came along to split man once again into a mind and a body joined by only the most tenuous and mysterious connection, the ground for the attack was already well prepared.

From the dualism of Descartes it was only a step to David Hume. Descartes had a nostalgia for the old order, as Beckett shows us in "Whoroscope," his early poem on Descartes, and tried to keep man, if not a union of mind and body, at least a mechanical assemblage of the two.[21] Some of his followers, such as Arnold Geulincx, a favorite of Beckett's Murphy and Molloy,[22] developed a school known as Occasionalism, based on the theory that the mental and physical systems run on separate but parallel tracks : we do not feel the heat of the flame, but we do feel a mental impression of heat precisely at the time the physical hand draws near the fire. The trouble with a dualism of this sort is that it offers no reason except an emotional one for continuing to believe that the external material world exists at all. Bishop Berkeley, another figure who lies in the background of Beckett's works,[23] pointed this out, but even he wanted to retain some belief in the objective reality of sense experience; he did not believe in the external existence of material objects, but he did argue from the truthfulness of God to the idea that an orderly stream of mental sense impressions under divine control constituted a kind of objective reality. David Hume was the first thinker in the modern world to carry this line of analysis to its logical conclusion.

Using a combination of Descartes's method of systematic doubt and the empiricism of John Locke, Hume analyzed all of man's basic traditional assumptions until there was nothing left of them. Substance fell apart under his eye into a multiplicity of impressions connected only by a habit of mind; causality reduced to a purely mental association of two things perceived as contiguous in space and time, *post hoc ergo propter hoc;* and even the self, the *res cogitans* which Descartes held to be the one rock-solid certainty, dissolved into an assortment of fragmentary impulses and ideas.

Beckett's novels and shorter works of fiction recapitulate these developments in modern thought. Most of his characters are fascinated by Dante's vision of unity, but they realize more or less clearly, depending on the case, that it is lost forever. Consequently they look for other explanations of existence, trying one after another and abandoning them as their inadequacies become unavoidably apparent. Like all men, they resent being deprived of certainty and cling to each set of ideas as long as they can. Murphy longs to become like Dante's Belacqua in the antepurgatory of the *Purgatorio,*[24] but since this is not a condition accessible to man in the flesh he seeks deliverance from this world through a mysticism made up of Pythagoreanism and Cartesian dualism. The book makes it quite clear that all of this is wishful thinking on Murphy's part. The quest of Watt, in *Watt,* for the vision of Knott parallels that of Dante for the vision of God, but in Watt's case the vision is shattering : Knott, when finally seen, has no definite shape, but changes his entire appearance continually from moment to moment.[25]

The trilogy — *Molloy, Malone Dies,* and *The Unnamable*[26] — traces the careers of several closely related characters, perhaps successive embodiments of a single consciousness, as they are driven from naïve acceptance of conventional thought to the most radical uncertainty. Moran, the least disillusioned of the group when we first see him, is, like Dante, a Catholic, but during the course of his story, his vision of the universe shifts from Dantesque to Kafka-esque. Molloy and Malone are relatively further along the path of disillusionment, but even they retain a belief in the existence of the self and, to a lesser degree, in the freedom of the will. The Unnamable, at the beginning of his volume, finds himself in a kind of after-death state in which he can no longer move about but can only think. He decides to pass the time by telling stories. As he becomes bored with the stories and tries to stop telling them and to stop thinking about possible explanations for his condition — what kind of place this is, who is in control of it, what is expected of him, and so on — he comes to realize that he has no control at all over his thoughts. The stories and speculations are simply there, in his mind. And as he reflects further on all of this, even the mind that they are in ceases to seem a certainty; he knows only that thoughts are there, not that they are his. The vision he ends with is very close to that of David Hume. In fact, although it was written two hundred years ago, Hume's description of the mind in his discussion of personal identity is a perfect commentary on the condition of the Unnamable :

The mind is a kind of theatre, where several perceptions successively make their appearance; pass, re-pass, glide away, and mingle in an infinite variety of postures and situations. There is properly no *simplicity* in it at one time, nor *identity* in different; whatever natural propension we may have to imagine that simplicity and identity. The comparison of the theatre must not mislead us. They are the successive perceptions only, that constitute the mind; nor have we the most distant notion of the place, where these scenes are represented, or of the materials, of which it is compos'd.[27]

This devastating vision was the logical outcome of the Cartesian critique of the medieval adaptation of Aristotle. Another movement that began as a rebellion against the medieval world-view and that might seem at first glance to have succeeded in establishing for man a secure position in the universe is that of modern science. In its own way, however, this movement too has contributed to the uprootedness of twentieth-century man.

The development of the science of mechanics in the later Middle Ages by such men as Roger Bacon, Thomas Bradwardine, and John Buridan posed no particular threat to the anthropocentric orientation that characterized the medieval world-view, but what really shattered that picture of things was the heliocentric revolution in astronomy led by Copernicus, Kepler, and Galileo, that "vile old Copernican lead-swinging son of a sutler" as Beckett's Descartes calls him in "Whoroscope." This movement began as a conscious attempt on the parts of Copernicus and Kepler to revive the Pythagorean worship of geometrical proportion; in fact Kepler even worked out an elaborate analysis of the harmony of the spheres, complete with musical scales.[28] They optimistically expected that this would provide man with a cosmology that would be simple, symmetrical, and beautiful.

This hope has not been borne out, however. The movement the neo-Pythagoreans began has gone on to revive in various ways the other ancient philosophies of atomism and hylozoism as well, and the final result has been the development in the twentieth century of a cosmology in which the old absolutes of space and time are reduced to relativities, and of an atomic physics in which particles can no longer be distinguished from waves, or, in Aristotelian terms, in which substance can no longer be distinguished from accident.[29]

Man in our age is the heir to centuries of analysis which have left experience in fragments and man a stranger in an unintelligible universe. The literature of the absurd is an expression of the state of mind to which this situation gives rise. We are impelled by our nature to seek understanding, but reason, the only instrument we have with which to seek it, has proven a clumsy and fragile tool. Beckett's Unnamable speaks for many when he describes the frustration of having to try forever to understand the unintelligible : "That the impossible should be asked of me, good, what else could be asked of me? But the absurd! Of me whom they have reduced to reason."[30]

It is out of this vision that Beckett has had to try to create art.

To do this means to attempt something nearly impossible : to embody in form a presentation of the formlessness of human experience in the twentieth century. Beckett is not the only writer who has felt the impact of this dilemma. Joyce and Céline in the 1920's and 1930's were wrestling with the same problem. In the 1940's while Beckett was working on *Watt,* the novels of the trilogy, and *Waiting for Godot,*[31] Thomas Mann, in his *Doctor Faustus,* was telling the story of a composer who, finding that all of human culture had degenerated into cliché, tried singlehandedly to achieve a "breakthrough" into a new vision which would make art once again possible.

In 1949, even as he was in the process of creating some of his greatest works, Beckett seems to have felt that the entire endeavor was futile. "To be an artist is to fail," he wrote in an essay on the paintings of his friend, Bram van Velde.[32] Van Velde, said Beckett, had become an abstract painter because representational painting was impossible : there was no longer a reality to represent. Traditional art had become reduced to a sequence of stubborn but futile attempts to adjust to a reality that had long since disappeared, "in a kind of tropism towards a light as to the nature of which the best opinions continue to vary, and with a kind of Pythagorean terror, as though the irrationality of pi were an offense against the deity, not to mention his creature."[33]

Van Velde, he says, succeeded in desisting from this automatism and in submiting to "the incoercible absence of relation."[34] Van Velde's solution was not, however, available to Beckett. A painter can turn to pure abstraction. So can a sculptor or a musician. But a writer cannot. The art of literature is inextricably tangled in the thicket of concrete experience. Beckett could only continue trying "to find a form that accommodates the mess."[35]

His achievement in this endeavor has been remarkable. In his novels and stories, from *More Pricks Than Kicks* to *The Unnamable* and *How It Is,* he has presented a carefully developed, progressive explication of his vision of "the mess." This is what gives his fiction as a whole such unusual continuity and overall coherence. The plays have continued the presentation of this picture, but in several cases, especially in the later plays, they have also gone on to attempt still more. The vision of the mess, if completely acquiesced in, would be only a dead end, and this is what it finally came to appear in the novels. Beckett himself said in an interview

in 1956 that in the fiction after *The Unnamable* he was having difficulty moving forward to something that would be more than a mere
repetition of what the previous work had already completely ex-
plored.[36] In this instance he was speaking of *Texts for Nothing*, but
the same problem is evident in *How It Is*. The plays reach out in
two principal directions in an attempt to carry his art beyond the
impasse to which *The Unnamable* had brought it. One of these is
that with which *How It Is* also experimented : that of the exploitation of form more or less for its own sake. The other is that of
continued exploration, the attempt to diagnose more adequately the
causes of our failure and to find a way beyond it. This seems to
have been what Beckett meant when he said to Tom Driver, "The
only chance of renovation is to open our eyes and see the mess."[37]
His work may picture despair, but it does not merely indulge it.
Despair is a part of the reality of our time, and as an honest artist
Beckett has had to be faithful to this reality. To find a way beyond
the absurd, one can only pass through it. Beckett's plays attempt to
do this.

CHAPTER II

Waiting for Godot

> I placed a jar in Tennessee,
> And round it was, upon a hill.
> It made the slovely wilderness
> Surround that hill.
>
> Wallace Stevens,
> "The Anecdote of the Jar"

Being, as Aristotle said, a creature that desires to know, man cannot endure for long the absence of meaning. And meaning, in its most basic sense, is pattern. If man cannot find pattern in his world, he will try by any means at his disposal to create it, or at least to imagine it. If a jar is not available, then a stump or a tin can will do. *Waiting for Godot* is the story of two vagabonds who impose on their slovenly wilderness an illusory, but desperately defended, pattern : waiting. The Godot they wait for is a vague figure at best and would probably be a disappointment to them if he came, but as long as they can make themselves believe that he will someday come and that he offers some kind of hope, they can comfort themselves with the thought that "in this immense confusion one thing alone is clear. We are waiting for Godot to come" (*Godot*, p. 51a).

The situation is a universal one. The only thing that distinguishes Vladimir and Estragon from Pozzo, Lucky, and the rest of us is that, having long since been deprived of most of the customary patterns that man imposes on his world, such as ownership and philosophical systems, they are forced to concentrate with a special intensity all their hope on this last illusion. Distilled in this way to its essentials, their situation becomes a symbol of that of man as such. They are man seeking meaning in an absurd universe. When asked who they are by Pozzo in Act II, Vladimir answers, "We are men" (p. 53). And in Act I Estragon had responded to the same question with

26

essentially the same answer: "Adam" (p. 25).[1] In the latter part of the play even Pozzo, after he has lost most of the possessions and powers that gave him personal identity and security, is universalized in the same way: when he answers to both "Cain" and "Abel," Estragon comments, "He's all humanity" (p. 54).

Vladimir and Estragon, representing a sort of composite Every-man, embody complementary aspects of human nature: Vladimir the intellectual side of man, Estragon the corporeal. Their names suggest their personalities. "Vladimir," for example, means "ruler of the world,"[2] a name that suggests the aspiration of intellect to master the universe by reducing it to knowledge, while "Estragon," the French word for the herb, tarragon, is a fitting name for a character so earthbound and with such persistent physical appetites. The way their personalities complement each other is reflected in a variety of characteristics. Vladimir has trouble with his hat, Estragon with his shoes. Vladimir has "stinking breath," Estragon "stinking feet" (p. 31). Estragon asks for carrots and radishes and is eager to hang himself when he hears that it will give him an erection. Vladimir, on the other hand, while not immune to physical appetite, tends to be more concerned with problems of meaning. For this reason he is also more optimistic; being more of a thinker, he has a greater need to search for explanations and to fabricate hopes. There is a significant irony in the fact that Vladimir, though the more intellectual of the two, is the less adequately intelligent: not as much of a thinker, Estragon has somewhat less need of knowledge and hope and is consequently somewhat less susceptible to illusions. Because he is more willing to let a mystery remain mysterious, he can retain a better grasp on reality. It is characteristic, for example, that when Vladimir is wrestling with the discrepancies among the four evangelists on the subject of the two thieves, Estragon's response is, "Well? They don't agree and that's all there is to it" (p. 9a). He can rest in an ignorance that would be intolerable to Vladimir, and in most of the circumstances with which this play deals a voluntarily accepted ignorance is the only reasonable attitude.

Pozzo and Lucky, in a more limited way, are also archetypal figures representing certain aspects of man.[3] One might describe their relationship as that of exploiter and exploited, keeping in mind that these terms must be understood in their most general senses. It is true, of course, that Pozzo is a landowner and slaveowner and that Lucky is his slave, but it would be much too simple to reduce them to symbols of an economic relationship, as Bertolt Brecht wished to do :[4] there are other equally significant types of exploitation involved. Pozzo, for example, can be interpreted as a symbol of the mass audience controlling and debasing the arts (since Lucky is a dancer) or as a nonintellectual world using thought as a plaything (since Lucky is a philosopher and theologian). And it should not be forgotten that Lucky is as attached to the relationship as Pozzo is : Lucky, Pozzo says, is trying to impress him so that he will keep him (p. 21), and he weeps when Pozzo speaks of getting rid of him. Although their relationship has proved a disappointment to both, they seem each to have believed at one time that it would bring them benefits. Pozzo says that Lucky used to think and dance "very prettily" once (p. 26a), though now he shudders at the thought of having to watch or listen to him. There was a time when Lucky used to dance "the farandole, the fling, the brawl, the jig, the fandango and even the hornpipe" (p. 27), but now all he dances is "the Net," a representation of his feeling of being trapped or entangled; and whereas Pozzo first took Lucky on nearly sixty years earlier in the hope of learning from him "beauty, grace, truth of the first water" (p. 22a), Lucky's thought has long since fallen into torturing incoherence.[5] Evidently this is the fate of art and thought in an absurd universe. We are not told exactly what Lucky was looking for when he entered the relationship, but since he is currently so intent on keeping his position with Pozzo, it would seem likely that what he was looking for was precisely his condition of servitude. Freedom is a difficult burden to bear in an absurd world, and many of Beckett's characters flee from it in a variety of ways; in the midst of chaos, slavery can appear to have something satisfyingly definite about it.

If this is the case, then the relationship of Pozzo and Lucky is a devastating comment on the hopes of Vladimir and Estragon. Since they have made their Godot into a kind of absolute authority, at least in their imaginations, their relationship to him, like Lucky's to Pozzo, is that of slaves :

Estragon : Where do we come in? . . .
Vladimir : Come in? On our hands and knees.
Estragon : As bad as that?
Vladimir : Your Worship wishes to assert his prerogatives?

Estragon : We've no rights any more? . . . We've lost our rights?
Vladimir : (*distinctly*). We got rid of them.

[pp. 13-13a]

If what they seek from Godot is what Lucky has already found, then
the emptiness of their hope is obvious, at least to the audience. Fortu-
nately for their peace of mind, however, it is not obvious to them.

Their situation, then, is that of people waiting for nothing much,
in a universe that has nothing much to offer. As they wait, and we
watch, we learn something about how man behaves under such circumstances. We see them devising, with diminishing success, games
to play to pass the time; we see them try again and again to understand the unintelligible; we see them discuss committing suicide,
but never without finding an excuse to put it off; we see them cling
to each other for company while continually bickering and talking
about how much better off they would be apart.

From their relationship we learn how inevitably isolated man is
within himself. Even though the company of one another is one of
the few distractions they have from the boredom and anxiety that
constantly press upon them, their moments of real companionship
are evanescent. Most of the time they are locked away from each
other in separate streams of thought. The mind is not only an in-
effective instrument of understanding, it is also a prison; man's
need to think merely aggravates his basic egocentricity. This is
made clear at the very beginning of the play. The scene opens with
Estragon seated on a mound struggling with a boot that will not
come off. Giving up temporarily he says, "Nothing to be done."
Vladimir hears this, but instead of asking what is wrong or if he can
help, he uses the words as a springboard for general philosophical
observations : "I'm beginning to come round to that opinion. All
my life I've tried to put it from me saying, Vladimir, be reasonable,
you haven't tried everything. And I resumed the struggle" (p. 7).
It takes some time for Estragon to get through to him, and when
they finally do get onto the same subject, Vladimir again uses it as
an occasion for a philosophical maxim : "Boots must be taken off
every day" (p. 7a). And sympathy has an even more difficult time
reaching between egos than does understanding :

Estragon : (*feebly*). Help me !
Vladimir : It hurts?

Estragon : (*angrily*). Hurts ! He wants to know if it hurts !
Vladimir : (*angrily*). No one ever suffers but you. I don't count.
I'd like to hear what you'd say if you had what I
have.

[p. 7a]

What Vladimir has seems to be gonorrhea, since it makes urination
difficult and painful for him. As Estragon continues to ask for help,
Vladimir continues to talk about his own problem, until finally
Estragon gets the boot off by himself.

Their reactions to the arrival of the blind Pozzo in Act II present
another illustration of the same tendency. When they hear Pozzo
and Lucky approaching, Estragon shouts, "God have pity on me !"
Vladimir, vexed, says, "And me?" but Estragon cries again, "On
me ! On me ! Pity ! On me !" (p. 49a). Then, after Pozzo falls and
calls for help and they have spent several minutes discussing
whether or not they would gain anything by helping him, Vladimir,
even in the process of resolving to go to Pozzo's aid, becomes so
lost in his own thoughts that he forgets all about Pozzo (pp. 51-52).
Although here in need of others, Pozzo himself during the first act,
when he was still secure in the power that his possessions and health
gave him, was even more impervious to communication than Vladimir and Estragon. He would wander off into long digressions while
they had to repeat their questions over and over again, trying to
catch him at a moment when he would be "on the alert" (p. 20).

Seeing the difficulty these characters have in communicating with
each other, one is reminded of what Malone said of Mr. and Mrs.
Saposcat in *Malone Dies* : "They had no conversation properly
speaking. They made use of the spoken word in much the same way
as the guard of a train makes use of his flags, or of his lantern."[6]
Even when their trains of thought are going in the same direction,
which is seldom enough, they run on separate, though parallel,
tracks.

Under ordinary circumstances the workings of the mind, even if
they reinforce man's basic isolation, do provide some comfort :
thought can be used to organize experience into patterns. The kinds
of pattern vary somewhat depending on the mind. Vladimir finds a
degree of serenity in the kind of thought that can be formulated
into maxims, and even Estragon, though less inclined to speculate,
can enjoy now and then an idea with a nice shape to it. The latter,

"aphoristic for once," says, "We are all born mad. Some remain so" (p. 51a). That the idea does not mean anything is less important than that it sounds as if it does. Pozzo, in better control of things in the first act than the two vagabonds, reduces reality to submission by imposing patterns of ownership on it. The trouble is, however, that in the universe Beckett portrays circumstances never remain ordinary for very long. The mind can never manage indefinitely to keep ahead of reality. The real plot of this play is the story of the gradual breakdown of all the illusory patterns that appear to give meaning to experience.

The illusion of ownership is probably the most fragile of these. Vladimir and Estragon were deprived of all but a few remnants of it long before the play began. Although they still have their clothing and are particularly attached to their hats and boots, and although Estragon is too keen on his carrot not to run back and get it when he drops it in his fright at the arrival of Pozzo and Lucky in Act I, these are only a few remaining vestiges of ownership. The archetypal representative of man's desire for possession is Pozzo. When he enters the first time with his slave, Lucky, loaded down with belongings of his, he is incensed to find the two vagabonds waiting on his land and thinks it "a disgrace" that the road is free to all (p. 16). As the act goes on, however, the security of ownership gradually slips away from him as his possessions disappear, one by one. His pipe, for example, and his watch simply vanish. This is a blow to his illusion of power, but although it distresses him that he is unable to find these things, he manages in the first act to avoid the full realization of what is happening. Giving up the search for his watch, he comforts himself with the thought that he "must have left it at the manor" (p. 31), though he had been making a conspicuous display of it only a few minutes earlier. Old habits of thought are a great comfort and an important defense against the direct vision of reality — "Habit is a great deadener," as Vladimir says at a later point (p. 58a) — and Pozzo clings to them as long as he can.[7] Even in Act II, when time has already eroded most of the power Pozzo once had, Pozzo still refers to Lucky as "my menial" (p. 56), and though the possessions that once filled the bags Lucky carries are now replaced by sand, Pozzo still drives him on.

As the various meanings that have given shape and coherence to their lives gradually fail them, all of the characters are forced to confront at least briefly, before finding new defenses or patching together the old ones, the real absurdity of existence. When they do, their world falls apart for them into a meaningless flux. "Everything oozes," says Estragon at one point, recalling Heraclitus's river of becoming, "It's never the same pus from one second to the next" (p. 39).

Even at the beginning of the first act the realization of absurdity is already beginning to be a threat. This is why Vladimir is so concerned over the problem of what became of the two thieves. When he tries to interest Estragon in the subject, he speaks of it as a game that will "pass the time" (p. 9), but it soon becomes evident that the mystery of the thieves is more than a mere game to him. There is a note of real perplexity, even perhaps anxiety, in his persistence in exploring it. The fate of the thieves, one of whom was saved and the other damned according to the one of the four accounts that "everybody" believes, becomes as the play progresses a symbol of the condition of man in an unpredictable and arbitrary universe. Various other situations echo it, gradually augmenting its significance. Pozzo, for example, says of Lucky's condition of servitude, "Remark that I might just as well have been in his shoes and he in mine. If chance had not willed otherwise" (p. 21a). Lucky has had luck all right, but the wrong kind. And Godot, who is kind to one boy but beats the other, is as arbitrary as God was to the thieves or to Cain and Abel.

As long as thought can find at least an illusion of meaning it is a source of some comfort, but the trouble is that it continually runs up against such ultimate mysteries as that represented by the story of the thieves. When this happens, the effect is not only disorienting but painful, sometimes excruciating. Lucky's speech and the response of the others to it is a good example. The very problem to which the story of the thieves refers seems to have had a great deal to do with the breakdown of Lucky's mind. The speech begins with the subject of "a personal God . . . with white beard . . . who from the heights of divine apathia divine athambia divine aphasia loves us dearly with some exceptions for reasons unknown but time will tell . . ." (p. 28a). The "time will tell" is wishful thinking, of course, and there is much wishful thinking in the speech : Lucky hopes that God suffers in sympathy "with those who for reasons unknown but time will tell are plunged in torment plunged in fire" and that he will one day "blast hell to heaven." A God who has already been defined as unable to feel, be impressed, or speak is supposed to care what becomes of man. In the universe of this play, time not only does not resolve such paradoxes, it continually forces them upon man's attention. The remainder of the speech shows both the persistence of Lucky's hope and the perplexity and despair to which the failure of his specific hopes is reducing him.

From the theological beginning he moves on to the subject of "Anthropopometry," in which it has been proved "beyond all doubt all other doubt than that which clings to the labors of men," proved, that is, with the most uncertain certainty but with irresistible force, "that man . . . in spite of the strides of alimentation and defecation wastes and pines wastes and pines" (p. 29). Human progress, that is, has not helped. Man's decay continues as steadily as ever in spite of dietetics and "what is more for reasons unknown in spite of the strides of physical culture the practice of . . . tennis, football, running . . . sports of all sorts."

From the study of man, Lucky proceeds to nature and the philosophies that have explained it. The four elements of Empedocles dissolve on the one hand into Heraclitean "rivers running water running fire" (p. 29a) and on the other into the entropy of death : ". . . and then the earth namely the air and then the earth in the great cold the great dark the air and the earth abode of stones in the great cold alas alas." And this "in spite of the tennis."

As the speech approaches its end, the image of a dying earth becomes a vast Golgotha : ". . . abode of stones . . . the skull the skull . . . the skull alas the stones." Lucky's last word, the opposite of Christ's, is "unfinished." The condition of a man is implicitly, whether Lucky realizes it consciously or not, a crucifixion. The only important difference between the agony of modern man and that of Christ is, as Estragon says somewhat later, that in the earlier time "they crucified quick" (p. 34a). In our time it is more drawn out, and less dramatic. "To every man his little cross," as Vladimir says, "Till he dies. . . . And is forgotten" (p. 40).

During the course of the speech, the three listeners become increasingly agitated until finally they throw themselves on Lucky and silence him. Pozzo has heard it all before, probably often, and therefore is "dejected and disgusted" (p. 28) at the start. Vladimir and Estragon are curious in the beginning because thought, at least in such a systematic form, is not quite so familiar to them. Although they occasionally touch on areas of mystery, they normally avoid going into them too far. Most of the time, as they tell us in Act II,

B

they use talk as a distraction so that they "won't think" (p. 40) and "won't hear. . . . All the dead voices" (p. 40a) of those who have thought before. When they do hear them, the world becomes "a charnel-house" (p. 41a) filled with the "corpses" of old ideas. Lucky's speech is a window into the charnel house, and the vision proves intolerable.

Silencing Lucky, conversing, and playing games can hold off for a while the realization of the futility of thought, but in the long run reality is more powerful than all man's defenses. "Time will tell," says Lucky, and it does, but in an entirely different sense from that which he intended. Ideas are necessary to man if he is to order his experience, but time eventually erodes even the most apparently solid ideas. The effect on man is slow torture. If ideas were demolished instantaneously and irretrievably, the process would be far less painful; meaninglessness would at least be something definite. Instead, however, man is continually teased with meanings that seem always just beyond his reach. This torment was something that Beckett's Watt knew well. After he had been living for some time in the household of the amorphous Mr. Knott, Watt found that things and the ideas that describe them began to slip apart. In the case of a pot, for example, he found that "it resembled a pot, it was almost a pot, but it was not a pot of which one could say, Pot, pot and be comforted."[8] Nor could one rest comfortably in the idea that it was not a pot. Potness hovered about it and would neither settle on it nor withdraw. "And it was just this hairbreadth departure from the nature of a true pot that so excruciated Watt." In their more perceptive moments, Vladimir and Estragon know the same feeling. "This is becoming really insignificant," says Vladimir at one point (p. 44). "Not enough," answers Estragon.

Most of the time, however, they are not even this conscious of the true nature of their problem. Normally, when they are not diverting themselves with superficial conversation, they spend their time trying to reduce the amorphous to form. Like Watt in the days before Knott, they stumble "in the midst of substance shadowy" pursuing certainties that always elude them.[9] Since Vladimir has the greater compulsion to think and understand, he is the more persistent and the more tormented of the two. When pattern breaks down, he is the one who feels it most keenly.

One of the seemingly most stable of the patterns that give shape to experience, and one of the most disturbing to see crumble, is that of time. Like the mystery of the thieves, this is a subject that is beginning to trouble Vladimir when the play opens, and as the action progresses it comes to seem more and more problematic, driving him finally to a crisis of realization.

The trouble begins when Estragon asks Vladimir what they did the day before. Vladimir has been insisting that they were someplace else doing something else, but he can't say where or what. When Estragon insists on being told, Vladimir bursts out angrily, "Nothing is certain when you're about" (p. 10a). Estragon then asks if Vladimir is sure that this is the evening they were to wait for Godot.

Vladimir : He said Saturday. (*Pause*) I think.
Estragon : You think.
Vladimir : I must have made a note of it. . . .
Estragon : (*very insidious*). But what Saturday? And is it Satur-
           day? Is it not rather Sunday? . . . Or Monday? . . .
           or Friday?
Vladimir : (*looking wildly about him, as though the date was in-
           scribed in the landscape*). It's not possible!
Estragon : Or Thursday?
Vladimir : What'll we do?

[pp. 10a-11]

In the face of these questions reality begins to fall apart into a dreamlike incoherence that Vladimir cannot endure. This may be why he refuses a minute later to listen to Estragon tell about a dream. "This one is enough for you?" asks Estragon (p. 11).

Pozzo, as one might expect, is as attached to an orderly time scheme as he is to his possessions, and in Act I he is still in a position to resist the doubts that are beginning to gnaw at Vladimir. He has a watch and a schedule and holds firmly to them. When Vladimir says, "Time has stopped," Pozzo cuddles his watch to his ear and replies, "Don't you believe it, Sir, don't you believe it. . . . Whatever you like, but not that" (p. 24a). Although he does not realize it at the time, when his watch later disappears it is more than just a possession that is slipping away from him.

After Pozzo and Lucky leave, Vladimir turns to Estragon and remarks on how they've changed. Estragon, however, says he doesn't know them. Vladimir, disturbed at the implications of this statement, insists that they do. But the seeds of doubt have been planted again : "Unless they're not the same . . ." he says to himself several times (p. 32).

This musing is cut short by the arrival of the boy, who comes to tell them that Godot will not come that evening "but surely to-morrow" (p. 33a), and who in his own turn contributes to the undermining of Vladimir's certainties.

> Vladimir : I've seen you before haven't I?
> Boy : I don't know, Sir.
> Vladimir : You don't know me?
> Boy : No Sir.
> Vladimir : It wasn't you came yesterday?
> Boy : No Sir.
> Vladimir : This is your first time?
> Boy : Yes Sir.
>
> [pp. 33-33a]

"Words words," says Vladimir after a silence. Words, the vehicles of man's ideas, no longer seem to fit reality.

If Act I raises doubts about the orderly relationship between the present and the past, Act II demolishes temporal pattern altogether. The stage directions read *"Next day. Same time. Same place"* (p. 36a), but during the act Vladimir is confronted with a variety of changes far too great to have taken place in one day's time. When the scene opens, Vladimir enters *"agitatedly"* (p. 37), perhaps because the absence of Estragon has left him too long to his own thoughts, and perhaps also because he has not quite recovered from the disorientation of the day before. Immediately he stops and "looks long" at the tree, which had been bare the day before (see p. 10) but which now "has four or five leaves." This evidently disturbs him, because it sets him moving *"feverishly"* about the stage, apparently looking for Estragon either as a source of distraction or as someone who can confirm that it is indeed the next day, same time, same place.

This feverish activity culminates in his singing loudly a song which has great significance as a foreshadowing of the vision of time which will force itself upon him before the play is over. He sings it by fits and starts, stopping now and then to brood as its significance perhaps breaks through to him. Reduced to its simple form it has a clearly cyclical pattern :

A dog came in the kitchen
And stole a crust of bread,
Then cook up with a ladle
And beat him till he was dead.

Then all the dogs came running
And dug the dog a tomb
And wrote upon the tombstone
For the eyes of dogs to come :

A dog came in the kitchen. . . .

The song starts over again where it began and repeats itself end-lessly. Time in the song is not a linear sequence, but an endlessly reiterated moment, the content of which is only one eternal event : death.

When Estragon finally arrives, Vladimir has company once more and a chance to try to reconstruct his time scheme. He first tries to get Estragon to confirm that this is the same place they were in the night before :

Vladimir : . . . . Do you not recognize the place?
Estragon : (*suddenly furious*). Recognize ! What is there to recog-nize? All my lousy life I've crawled about in the mud ! And you talk to me about scenery ! . . . Look at this muckheap ! I've never stirred from it !

[p. 39a]

The reply, of course, not only does nothing to reassure Vladimir as to the place, but also implies that just as there is only one place, the mud, so there is only one time, that of the life in the mud.[10]

Vladimir then attempts to reconstruct, if not the day before, then the larger scheme of the past, but with no more success. He tries to remind Estragon of the time some years before when they were grape pickers in the Macon country, but even he cannot remember the name of the man they worked for and Estragon insists that he was never there : "I've puked my puke of a life away here, I tell you ! Here ! In the Cackon country" (p. 40).[11] *Cackon* is a pun on the French word *caca,* a child's word for excrement.[12] Once again what Estragon means is that all he has known of the world has been mud or something even more unpleasant.

After a little further conversation, during which Estragon asks Vladimir to "sing something" (p. 41) and he refuses — the song seems to have disturbed him, since his response, "No no!", suggests a horror of beginning it again — Vladimir finally remembers that he wanted to ask Estragon how he would account for the change in the tree : ". . . yesterday evening it was all black and bare. And now it's covered with leaves. . . . In a single night" (p. 42a). "It must be the Spring," says Estragon. "But in a single night!" Vladimir insists. Estragon answers that they were somewhere else the day before, that the problem is just another of Vladimir's "nightmares," and for a moment Vladimir feels reassured : "(*sure of himself*). Good. We weren't here yesterday evening. Now what did we do yesterday evening?" Estragon's reply to this question, however, echoes his earlier description of the place : "Yes, now I remember, yesterday evening we spent blathering about nothing in particular. That's been going on now for half a century." Vladimir is looking for a time scheme with some sort of fixed shape to it, but all he can get from Estragon is an eternal, formless mud and blather.

Things look as if they are going to take on a shape once again when Vladimir finds that Estragon does remember the kick Lucky gave him the previous day and even locates the wound, but the arrival of Pozzo and Lucky a little later destroys this tentatively recovered certainty. The changes that have taken place in them, like the foliation of the tree, are too great to be accounted for by the passage of twenty-four hours : Pozzo is now blind and decrepit, and Lucky is dumb. When he hears them coming, Vladimir naïvely hopes that the arrival of "reinforcements" (p. 49a) will deliver them from their stagnation and set time moving again : "Time flows again already. The sun will set, the moon rise" (p. 50). What happens, however, is quite the reverse.

Seeing the enormous change in Pozzo, Vladimir has to try to explain it, at least in the sense of pinning it down to a particular moment on a linear time scale. But when he asks Pozzo when it happened, he finds Pozzo even less firmly oriented in time than he :

Vladimir : I'm asking you if it came on you all of a sudden.
Pozzo :   I woke up one fine day as blind as Fortune. . . . Sometimes I wonder if I'm not still asleep.
Vladimir : And when was that?
Pozzo :   I don't know.

Vladimir : But no later than yesterday—
Pozzo :   (*violently*). Don't question me! The blind have no
            notion of time. The things of time are hidden from
            them too.

[p. 55a]

Pozzo tries rather feebly to recover some sense of time and place
himself — "Is it evening?" (p. 55), is this "by any chance the place
known as the Board?" (p. 55a) — but as Vladimir keeps insisting
that Pozzo confirm the relationship between today and yesterday,
he drives Pozzo finally to the vision both of them have been trying
to avoid :

Pozzo : (*suddenly furious*). Have you not done tormenting me with
        your accursed time! When! When! One day, is that not
        enough for you, one day he went dumb, one day I went
        blind, one day we'll go deaf, one day we were born, one
        day we shall die, the same day, the same second, is that
        not enough for you? . . . They give birth astride of a
        grave, the light gleams an instant, then it's night once
        more.

[p. 57a]

When time is seen in this way, an endless cycle of birth and death
repeating forever the same eternal moment, it ceases to have either
flow or direction but only, in the words of the Unnamable, "piles
up all about you, instant on instant" in seconds that are "all alike
and each one . . . infernal."[13]

Pozzo leaves at this point, and Vladimir is left to try to bolster
again his still more badly shaken sense of coherence. Waking Estragon, who slept through the preceding conversation, he tries out on
him the idea that perhaps Pozzo might not really have been blind,
that is, that he had not really changed so much from the day before. Estragon is as little help as ever. "You dreamt it," he says (p.
58), then asks if Vladimir is sure Pozzo is not Godot. "Not at all,"
answers Vladimir with certainty, but then, "(*Less sure*) Not at all!
(*Still less sure*) Not at all!" Giving up finally his attempts to understand what has happened and what is happening, he says, "I don't
know what to think any more." Then, as Estragon settles back into
sleep, Vladimir proceeds from this radical uncertainty to the vision
of cyclical time that Pozzo had introduced but that Vladimir had

till now resisted : "Astride of a grave and a difficult birth. Down
in the hole, lingeringly, the grave-digger puts on the forceps. We
have time to grow old" (p. 58). This is all that time is in this vision,
a moment in which to grow old and die, and to fill the air with
"our cries" (p. 58a).

At this point the boy comes in again, and this time Vladimir is
not surprised that the boy does not recognize him. He can even
anticipate his lines :

> Vladimir : You have a message from Mr. Godot.
> Boy : Yes Sir.
> Vladimir : He won't come this evening.
> Boy : No Sir.
> Vladimir : But he'll come tomorrow.
> Boy : Yes Sir.
>
> [p. 58a]

After a few questions about whether the boy had seen Pozzo and
Lucky or not and about the health of the boy's brother, Vladimir
asks a final question that proves shattering for him :

> Vladimir : (*softly*). Has he a beard, Mr. Godot?
> Boy : Yes Sir.
> Vladimir : Fair or . . . (*he hesitates*) . . . or black?
> Boy : I think it's white, Sir.
> *Silence.*
> Vladimir : Christ have mercy on us !
>
> [p. 59]

Evidently in this moment, having let down most of the defenses that
normally shield him from the vision of reality, he realizes the painful truth that the Godot he has made with his imagination into a
kind of God, into a figure, that is, representing absolute power and
ultimate meaning, is as empty a God as the traditional one "with
white beard" that Lucky described in his speech.

Such a realization is not easy to endure for long, however, and
Vladimir is no hero. He retreats from it almost immediately. When
Estragon awakes and suggests that they "go far away from here"
(p. 59a), Vladimir, reconstructing the old faith for both of them,
says they cannot go far because they have to come back again the
next day "to wait for Godot." And in what seems to be a further

attempt to rekindle his belief in the power of life he says, "Everything's's dead but the tree." This is not the first time they have tried to "turn resolutely towards Nature" (p. 41a), and it will probably not be the last. Even if time stands still, man cannot. Pozzo, after his vision of the emptiness and futility of human life, revives his Lucky and cries, "On!" though they have nowhere to go and nothing to carry but sand. Vladimir and Estragon too go on in their own way, but the critic must resist the temptation to interpret this as an affirmation on the part of the play of hope or human fortitude. All of these characters go on, but in the old ruts, and only by retreating into patterns of thought that have already been thoroughly discredited. In the universe of this play, "on" leads nowhere.

CHAPTER III

All That Fall

All That Fall,[1] which was first presented by the British Broadcasting Corporation on January 13, 1957, about three months before the premiere of *Endgame,* was Beckett's first radio play and also his first work written originally in English since the writing of *Watt,* a period of almost a decade. The return to English brought with it a return to more concrete settings, something that was to continue in subsequent English works, particularly *Krapp's Last Tape* and *Embers. Waiting for Godot* had had a rather vague, abstract locale, as had the novels of the trilogy, and as *Endgame,* another French work, was to have, but in *All That Fall* we find ourselves in a palpably realistic Irish rural village, Boghill, with dusty roads, houses, a railroad station, a race course, and a church.

In spite of the great difference in atmosphere, however, *All That Fall* is very closely related to both *Waiting for Godot* and *Endgame* in theme. Like *Godot* it is concerned with the question of the possibility of a meaningful life for man in a world in which meaning seems always to be slipping away from him, and like *Endgame,* as we shall see, it is concerned with a conflict between the forces of life and those of death.

In *All That Fall* these opposing forces are represented by the aged Maddy Rooney and her still more aged husband, Dan, as seen in their divergent reactions to various children. Maddy pines for the children she does not have, while her husband hates children and, from all indications, has probably just killed one at about the time the play begins. Their state of physical decay and their general disappointment with life unite them in a common disillusionment, exemplified when they *"join in wild laughter"* at Maddy's mention of the Biblical text from which the play receives its title : "The Lord upholdeth all that fall and raiseth up all those that be bowed down" (p. 88).[2] At the same time, however, their basic attitudes toward life are quite opposed. Dan has spent all his life impatiently dying, while Maddy, though often overcome by despair and consequently driven to thoughts of death, fundamentally has always been drawn toward life. Her problem has been not lack of desire to live, but the absence of conditions, both personal and in her social and cultural milieu, which would have enabled her to live a full life.

Dan has obviously been part of the problem. As he says, they tend to move in opposite directions : ". . . you forwards and I backwards. The perfect pair. Like Dante's damned, with their faces arsy-versy" (pp. 74-75).[3] Characteristically, it was Maddy who proposed to Dan, dragging him, at least as he described it, back into a life he had almost managed to escape from : "The day you proposed to me the doctors gave me up. You knew that, did you not? The night you married me they came for me with an ambulance" (p. 75). The relationship is very like that in *Murphy* between Murphy and his Celia, the last woman whose psychology Beckett portrayed in depth.[4] There one saw a similar conflict between a man who wanted to escape from the world and a woman who wanted to live in it and who needed him in order to do so. Murphy and Celia were much younger, of course, and Murphy managed to make his escape, or at least to stumble onto it — he was blown to pieces under circumstances that were never made completely clear — but the situation was essentially the same : Maddy and Dan are what Murphy and Celia might have become in old age if she had managed to marry him and get him settled down in a job as she had wished.

The story of *All That Fall* is the gradual unfolding of this situation, and since this is a radio play, much of this is communicated through sound effects. The first sounds we hear announce the themes and present the opposing forces of the play. First the sounds of animals, representing nature's vitality : *"Rural sounds. Sheep, bird, cow, cock, severally, then together"* (p. 33) — sounds that subsequently recur at various points in the play, always to contrast the fertility of nonhuman nature with the sterility of man. Then, after a silence, comes the sound of Maddy advancing along the country road toward the railroad station to meet her husband, the sound of her *"dragging feet"* symbolizing the afflictions of the human condition : age, decay, the intractability of the flesh. As Maddy moves along she hears another sound : *"Music faint from house by way. 'Death and the Maiden.'"* "Poor woman. All alone in that ruinous old house," says Maddy to herself. She stops to listen, the music grows louder, then fades away as Maddy walks on, humming the melody.

The symbolism of this music is very important to the play. It presents death as simultaneously an appealing escape and the destruction of possibility. The poem *Der Tod und das Mädchen* by Matthias Claudius, which served as the inspiration for Schubert's music, is a dialogue between tempting death and a tempted but fearful maiden :

Das Mädchen :   Vorüber ! Ach, vorüber !
                   geh, wilder Knochenmann !
                   Ich bin noch jung, geh, Lieber !
                   und rühre mich nicht an.
Der Tod :   Gib deine Hand, du schön und zart Gebild !
                   Bin Freund und komme nicht zu strafen.
                   Sei gutes Muts ! ich bin nicht wild,
                   sollst sanft in meinen Armen schlafen !

"Away, oh, go away, go, fierce man of bones," she says, "I am still young, go, *Lieber,* and touch me not !" *Lieber,* the term by which she addresses him, means "lover" or "dear one"; here it is both an entreaty and a term of endearment, reflecting her inner conflict with regard to the attraction death has for her. Death's answer is : "Give me your hand, young and tender creature ! I am a friend and do not come to injure you. Do not be afraid ! I am not fierce; you will sleep gently in my arms !" It is significant that the girl is a virgin, a potential vehicle of procreation, not yet a fulfilled woman. Death will be a solace for her, but will also deny her the possibility of developing into the full being of womanhood.

Maddy is another who has been deprived of this fulfillment. Like the woman all alone in the "ruinous old house," Maddy, in her aged body, is in ruins and alone. Long past child-bearing, she suffers continually from the thought of the child she never had, or perhaps had and lost. Every now and then she stops and laments for her "Minnie ! Little Minnie !" (pp. 37 and 42, for example), who if she had lived, or been born, would now be some forty or fifty years old and who would in her own turn "be girding up her lovely little loins, getting ready for the change" (p. 42).

Maddy's husband seems to have had a great deal to do with her barrenness, at least from the hints we get. It is obvious that with his hatred of children he would be unlikely to want her to have one, and from what she says it sounds as if he never did much to give her the opportunity :

> Love, that is all I asked, a little love, daily, twice daily, fifty years of twice daily love like a Paris horse-butcher's regular, what normal woman wants affection? A peck on the jaw at morning, near the ear, and another at evening, peck, peck, till you grow whiskers on you.
>
> [p. 37]

She probably never even received very many pecks; when she meets Dan at the station and asks him for a kiss, he is indignant : "Kiss you? In public? . . . Have you taken leave of your senses?" (p. 67).

Now she is already long past the time in her life when fertility would have made it possible for her to produce anything more than whiskers. There is no more future ahead of her. As she tells Christy, the carter, when he asks if she can use some of the dung he is taking to market, "What would we want with dung, at our time of life?" (p. 35). Others may be able to plan gardens, but there is nothing left for Maddy to await except death.

At the same time, however, the side of her nature that has been deprived of fulfillment is not ready to acquiesce in this sterility or to leave her in peace. At times it revives in the form of joy in the life of nature, as when she turns from thoughts of the pecks that produce only whiskers to say, "There is that lovely laburnum again" (p. 37). At other times it takes the form of an acute sexual anxiety. The eyes of Christy's hinny, the sterile hybrid of a she-ass and a stallion, torment her, as though she feels that the animal recognizes in her a sterility like its own. And when she meets Mr. Tyler a few moments later, her conversation with him has a strong undertone of frustrated sexuality. Mr. Tyler's playful attempt to flirt with her, by suggesting that he might be more steady on his bicycle if she allowed him to lay his hand lightly on her shoulders, triggers another outburst like that about pecks on the cheek : "No, Mr. Rooney, Mr. Tyler I mean, I am tired of light old hands on my shoulders and other senseless places, sick and tired of them" (p. 39). The slip she makes in calling Mr. Tyler "Mr. Rooney" is obviously significant, especially as she makes it again a few pages later (p. 42). She is expressing against Mr. Tyler the resentment she feels toward her husband for not providing her with the kind of love she has wanted. As they walk along, she hears the cooing of doves (p. 41), a mating call, and this reminds her of her lost Minnie, causing her to stop in the road and weep and finally to drive Mr. Tyler away. After he leaves, the cooing, repeated, provokes another explosion which lays bare her whole anguish.

> (*Cooing.*) Venus birds! Billing in the woods all the long summer long. (*Pause.*) Oh cursed corset! If I could let it out, without indecent exposure. Mr. Tyler! Mr. Tyler! Come back and unlace me behind the hedge! (*She laughs wildly, ceases.*) What's wrong with me, what's wrong with me, never tranquil, seething out of my dirty old pelt, out of my skull, oh to be in atoms, in atoms. (*Frenziedly.*) ATOMS!
>
> [p. 43]

Mr. Tyler, of course, would have been no more likely than her husband to provide Maddy with what she really wants, a genuine participation in the vitality of nature; he is himself as uninterested in life, even hostile to it, as Dan. He can make a joke of his daughter's hysterectomy — "They removed everything, you know, the whole . . . er . . . bag of tricks" (p. 38) — and at one point, when asked by Maddy what he is mumbling about, he answers, "I was merely cursing, under my breath, God and man, under my breath, and the wet Saturday afternoon of my conception" (p. 39).

A characteristic feature of men which contributes to their remoteness from the natural world in which Maddy would like to have a more active part is their tendency toward abstraction, the preference of the artificial and mechanical over that which is organic and alive. Dan, for example, prefers mental calculations, such as monetary computations or counting the steps at the station, to immediate experience. "Not count!" he says, "One of the few satisfactions in life?" (p. 71), in a scene in which Maddy is trying to persuade him to negotiate the steps in a concrete way rather than just calculate their number. "No, just cling to me and all will be well," she says, trying to call him back to herself and to the immediacy of life. Another example is Dan's tendency to be more interested in the etymologies of words and the laws that govern them — he mentions, for instance, the derivation of the Gaelic *fir* from the Latin *vir* in accordance with Grimm's Law (p. 82) — than in their value as instruments of communication. His idea of an ideal life would be to do nothing but sit, "counting the hours — till the next meal" (p. 72). And already blind, he would like to be deaf and dumb as well, totally cut off from the world of nature.

Mr. Tyler is not as much of a calculator as Dan, but he too is associated with the mechanical in the form of the bicycle he rides, and the next man Maddy meets after Mr. Tyler is Mr. Slocum in his automobile, the kind of "great roaring machine" (p. 41) that Maddy considers a nuisance. It is probably significant that Maddy has a hard time getting into the car when Mr. Slocum offers her a lift, succeeding only after great difficulty and at the expense of a torn frock, and that when they drive off with a grinding of gears, the car runs over a hen. "Oh mother, you have squashed her," says Maddy.

The failure of men to value natural life is not, however, the only source of the sickness of this world, nor is Maddy's inability to live only a state of being cut off from womanly fulfillment in mother-hood. The real problem with life, both for Maddy and for the other inhabitants of Boghill, is something much more fundamental and complex. One of Maddy's laments gives some indication of this : "Oh I am just a hysterical old hag I know, destroyed with sorrow and pining and gentility and church-going and fat and rheumatism and childlessness" (p. 37). It is significant that childlessness and physical decay are not the only afflictions she mentions; gentility and church-going are also among the forces that have destroyed her. The deepest problem of this world is a general failure both of Maddy and of the community of which she is a member to live on a level deeper than that of shallow conventionality. The kind of gentility that isolates people from one another, imprisoning them in civility, the kind of religious life that is concerned more with appearance than with any reality, in general the kind of timidity that inhibits any impulse toward individual thought and experi-ence — all of this is what reduces the life of Boghill to sterility. This is probably part of what Maddy means when she says at one point, "I am not half alive nor anything approaching it" (p. 41) — not only that her vitality has been reduced by age but also that she has never been more than fractionally alive.

Living evidence of the stifling power of convention in Boghill is Mr. Barrell, the station master. "How long have you been master of this station now Mr. Barrell?" asks Maddy.

Mr. Barrell :   Don't ask me, Mrs. Rooney, don't ask me.
Mrs. Rooney : You stepped into your father's shoes, I believe,
                when he took them off.
Mr. Barrell :   Poor Pappy! (*Reverent pause.*) He didn't live long
                to enjoy his ease.
Mrs Rooney :   I remember him clearly. A small ferrety purple-
                faced widower, deaf as a doornail, very testy and
                snappy. . . . I suppose you'll be retiring soon
                yourself, Mr. Barrell, and growing your roses.

                                                    [p. 52]

Mr. Barrell's choice of life, motivated by a combination of rever-
ence and lack of imagination, has made him into simply a carbon
copy of his father. That the likeness is complete, even down to the
testiness and snappiness, is shown by the *"backhanded blow in the
stomach"* (p. 59) that he gives to Tommy, his assistant, a bit later.

Probably the best example in the play of the deadening, pervert-
ing power of convention is Miss Fitt, the very embodiment
of "gentility and church-going." As the multiple pun in her name
suggests, she is both a misfit in the town, because of her abstracted-
ness and her indifference to others, and at the same time a perfect
fit, in that the very qualities that separate her from the other towns-
people are themselves only exaggerated, caricaturized versions of
the essential features of the life all of them share.

The first we hear of Miss Fitt is the sound of her voice humming
a hymn. She is so insulated in her pious revery that she takes no
notice of Maddy, who has to shout at her to be recognized : "Miss
Fitt! . . . Am I then invisible, Miss Fitt? Is this cretonne so becoming to me that I merge into the masonry?" (p. 54). When Maddy
reminds her that on the preceding Sunday they "worshipped together . . . knelt side by side at the same altar . . . drank from the
same chalice," Miss Fitt explains that in church she is "alone with
[her] Maker," so alone with him that she is oblivious to everything
around her, even — perhaps especially — the collection plate, and
that on weekdays as well she is always "distray, very distray" (p. 55).
She is never present to her world : "I suppose the truth is I am not
there, Mrs. Rooney, just not really there at all" (p. 55). Religion
for her is an escape into herself, and she is resentful if anyone tries
to violate her privacy. She becomes hysterical, for example, when
Maddy tries to join in her hymn with the words.

Insular, then, as her religious life is, it has little room in it for concern with others. When Maddy asks for help getting up the steps of the station, Miss Fitt's annoyance is barely concealed: "Is it my arm you want then? (*Pause. Impatiently.*) Is it my arm you want, Mrs. Rooney, or what is it?" (p. 57). "Your arm!" explodes Maddy, "Any arm! A helping hand! For five seconds!" When this sort of appeal to charity produces only a remonstrance that Maddy really should not be going about at all, she turns to a more effective weapon, conventional opinion: "Come down here, Miss Fitt, and give me your arm, before I scream down the parish!" This threat succeeds, where appeal to sympathy failed, in persuading Miss Fitt that "it is the Protestant thing to do." Even for her own mother, Miss Fitt has little feeling that goes beyond purely egocentric interests: thinking that the delay in the train's arrival may be the result of an accident, she expresses her concern in a manner which betrays its true focus: "Oh darling mother! With the fresh sole for lunch!" (p. 63).

Miss Fitt's use of religion as a withdrawal from life recalls the music, *Death and the Maiden,* and further unfolds its symbolism. Miss Fitt is another maiden who withdraws from the life of womanhood into a kind of death. That death is the conscious goal of her religious aspirations is quite obvious from her explanation of why she is so "distray": "I see, hear, smell, and so on . . . but my heart is not in it. . . . Left to myself, with no one to check me, I would soon be flown . . . home" (pp. 55-56). And it is characteristic that that the hymn she hums — Newman's "Lead Kindly Light" — should go, "The night is dark and I am far from ho-ome" (p. 58).

As it is, the life this religion gives "the dark Miss Fitt," as she is called both by herself and others (pp. 55, 59), is itself a kind of living death. She is already cut off from the life of nature in a perpetual maidenhood, physically wasted to "a bag of bones," as Maddy says (p. 58), and even her face has faded to obscurity:

Mr. Barrell : Who is that?
Tommy : The dark Miss Fitt.
Mr. Barrell : Where is her face?

[p. 59]

One reason religion has become moribund in Boghill is that meaning generally, not just religious meaning but any kind of meaning that is embodied in concepts and language, is dying. Miss Fitt does not see this, but it is something that repeatedly occurs to her more perceptive coreligionist, Maddy. One of the first things we hear Maddy say is that she is bothered by the inadequacy of words. "Do you find anything . . . bizarre about my way of speaking?" she asks Christy, "I do not mean the voice. . . . No, I mean the words. (*Pause. More to herself.*) I use none but the simplest words, I hope, and yet I sometimes find my way of speaking very . . . bizarre" (p. 35). Later, after having met Dan, when she uses some conventional phrases of the sort that imply that there is still a possibility the universe can be a home to man — "we shall press on and never pause, never pause, till we come safe to haven" (p. 80) — Dan points out that her language is made up of empty clichés: "Never pause . . . safe to haven . . . Do you know, Maddy, sometimes one would think you were struggling with a dead language." She answers that she often has that feeling herself and that it is excruciating. "Theirs has not changed, since Arcady," she says of a lamb crying to suck its mother, but English, "just like our own poor dear Gaelic," and like any human language, will soon be dead. Lambs, doves, cows, all the creatures of nature have the great advantage over man that they can live without meanings. Man cannot. He must have the mediation of words and ideas between himself and reality, and if he becomes aware of the emptiness of the words he uses, then he cannot avoid realizing that his entire mental life is empty as well. Dan and Maddy are both very close to this realization if they have not already reached it.

Most of the citizens of Boghill, however, are not so clear-sighted. Mr. Barrell can still believe in the importance of keeping his station well ordered; Tommy can still be concerned with finding a winning horse for the races; Miss Fitt can still believe in her caricature of salvation. Each can believe that appearances, respectability, power over one another, all that constitutes the life of "gentility," still have sufficient value to be worth worrying about. "Come, Dolly darling, let us take up our stand before the first-class smokers. Give me your hand and hold me tight, one can be sucked under," says one nameless female voice, concerned even in this admonition to let those around her know that her family is not the kind to travel by other than first-class cars. She does not realize that in taking her daughter's hand she is saving the child from one death only to deliver her to another.

A story Maddy tells Dan about the fate of another child reveals the full significance of this incident as well as further elaborating that of the *Death and the Maiden* motif. In a lecture by "one of these new mind doctors" (p. 82) — apparently a psychoanalyst — she had heard the story of a little girl whom the lecturer had treated unsuccessfully for years and who had nothing specifically wrong with her except that she was dying. The story in itself, says Maddy, would not seem especially significant if it had not been for something the man said afterwards which had "haunted" her ever since :

When he had done with the little girl he stood there motionless for some time, quite two minutes I should say, looking down at his table. Then he suddenly raised his head and exclaimed, as if he had had a revelation, The trouble with her was she had never really been born !

[p. 84]

The story is in microcosm the story of a whole world of little girls — Maddy, Miss Fitt, the female voice and her daughter — and of men as well, all of whom are languishing, "not half alive nor anything approaching it" (p. 41), reduced to the condition of "a big pale blur" (p. 56) by their failure or inability to be born as fully alive individuals. Many choose voluntarily to live shadow lives by limiting themselves to a superficial, collective identity, while others, such as Maddy, would like to break through the shell of cliché to a more vital existence, but find themselves shut off from it, perhaps by their own weakness, perhaps by the nature of things.

Whether human life could ever be possible in any fuller form than that of the inhabitants of Boghill is uncertain. Moran, in *Molloy*, when told that his boss, a vague God-like figure, had said life was a thing of beauty and a joy forever, asked, "Do you think he meant human life?" (*Molloy*, p. 226). This is a question that also troubles Maddy. "Can hinnies procreate, I wonder," she muses as she and Dan walk home, "You know, hinnies, or is it jinnies, aren't they barren, or sterile, or whatever it is?" (pp. 85-86). The question is more than academic, and even more than personal for her. She is thinking not only of the hinny that had stopped to stare at her earlier in the day, but also of another one that represents far more : "It wasn't an ass's colt at all, you know . . . it was a hinny, he rode into Jerusalem or wherever it was on a hinny. (*Pause*) That must mean something." If it does mean something, then the meaning is disheartening. If Christ, a traditional symbol of the wholeness of humanity and of the possibility of renewal, rode on a sterile beast, it would seem a wry joke on man's hope for renewed vitality. "It's like the sparrows, than many of which we are of more value, they weren't sparrows at all," she says. Sparrows, a traditional symbol of sexual vigor, are also taken away from her. "They weren't sparrows at all," she repeats with emotion. There is neither a Lord to uphold all that fall and raise up all those that be bowed down, nor is there even a life to raise them into.

The implication for the play as a whole is that the opposition between the forces of life and the forces of death is not necessarily a matter of ethical values. The association of Dan with the death of the child who fell off the train and the association of Maddy with the enjoyment of nature and a desire for fulfillment in motherhood might before close examination make it appear that she is to be thought of as morally good and Dan as morally evil. It is true, of course, that Dan is hostile to life. Whether Dan has actually murdered the child on the train or not — the circumstances are vague but sinister — he is obviously homicidal : "Did you ever wish to kill a child?" he asks Maddy at one point, "Nip some young doom in the bud. . . . Many a time at night, in winter, on the black road home, I nearly attacked the boy. . . . Poor Jerry," speaking of the boy he employs to guide him home. But if life is as devoid of possibility as it would seem, murder is not necessarily cruel and death is not necessarily an evil. Dan's hostility to life may proceed not from ill will, but rather from a clearer than usual perception of life's real hopelessness, and his expression of pity for "poor Jerry" may indicate that there is an element of altruism in his homicidal impulses. Perhaps as egocentric as we have seen him to be, he still has just this much sympathy for others left — to want to put them out of their misery.

The complexity of the question of life's value is communicated symbolically by a frequently recurring image : excrement. Manure, such as that which Christy offered Maddy at the beginning, is a source of fertility for nonhuman nature, but to man it is not very pleasant stuff. When Maddy Rooney — whose maiden name, Dunne (a pun on *dun* or *brown*), associates her as she was in her maidenhood with this image of potential fertility — fell into the ruin-y state that the play has shown to be the ultimate reality of all human life, her own life was left a "manure heap," as she calls it at one point (p. 71), and a barren one at that. Without its redeeming fertility, excrement is only excrement, Vladimir's tree and Maddy's laburnum may continue to bloom in the life of nonhuman nature, but in *All That Fall*, as in *Waiting for Godot*, man is still in what Estragon called "the Cackon country."

CHAPTER IV

Endgame

Waiting for Godot, which was written at the same time as the trilogy of novels — *Molloy, Malone Dies,* and *The Unnamable* — was essentially a dramatic presentation of the vision developed in those works.[1] In the trilogy the destiny of the three characters shows that "on," in that universe, leads nowhere. They journey on quests and even grow, at least in the sense of losing illusions, but the ultimate end of their development is the condition of the Unnamable, bewildered, lost, disillusioned completely with even the possibility of knowledge, but unable to stop talking to himself and trying to explain the inexplicable.[2] And *All That Fall,* though written approximately seven years later, reflects essentially the same vision of human life.

Endgame, however, is a new departure. This play does not provide answers any more than the earlier works did, but it leaves open the possibility that a new path out of the old ruts might lead, if one has the courage to walk it, to a new vision and a new life. Although it does not lead us on this quest, it points the way to it and prepares for it by exploring the moral and intellectual failures that currently imprison us.

Writing to his American director, Alan Schneider, in 1956 while he was still working on *Endgame,* Beckett described the new play as "rather difficult and elliptic, mostly depending on the power of the text to claw, more inhuman than 'Godot.' "[3] The reason it is so much more abrasive and inhuman than *Godot* is that, with more hope for what man might become, it is more brutal and unyielding in the way it probes into the etiology of our present condition. Vladimir and Estragon were isolated to a large degree in their egocentric preoccupations with their own thoughts and their own sufferings, but there was also an element of warmth in their relationship. They were frequently cruel to one another — as when Estragon tells the story of the Englishman in the brothel to torture Vladimir (*Godot,* p. 11a) — but they could also embrace and

54

make up. In a universe in which nothing was possible, company was at least a distraction and the play left them free to make of it what they could. In *Endgame,* on the other hand, the relationship between Hamm and Clov is part of the trap, and for there to be any hope, the trap must be seen through and broken out of.

The play is built around images of isolation and imprisonment. The scene opens upon two trash cans within another similar container, the room itself. The content of all the containers is refuse : Nagg and Nell in the two ashbins, Hamm and Clov in the room. The house is both a "shelter" (p. 3) and a place of isolation, in which old ways of thought, clung to out of fear or stubbornness, both protect the inhabitants and cut them off from the reality outside. *"High up"* on the rear wall are *"two small windows, curtains drawn"* (p. 1), which suggest that the room may represent the inside of the skull of a man who has closed his eyes to the external world.

Eva Metman has suggested that in Beckett's plays generally, "The various figures which he puts on the stage are not really persons but figures in the inner world," and in regard to *Endgame,* at least, there seems to be truth to this.[4] Nagg and Nell in their cans remind one of Proustian involuntary memories sealed in jars : Hamm frequently feels he would like to suppress the memory of them but it comes back to him apart from his volition as they emerge now and then from their cans to remind him of their existence.[5] And the dialogue of Hamm and Clov often seems like that of a mind with itself. To interpret the characters of the play as only symbols of psychological forces would be too simple by itself, however; Beckett's characters rarely seem to be *only* anything. They are probably this, seen in one respect, but they are also real individuals with real interactions that are significant.

At the center of the household, both literally and figuratively, is Hamm. He is the proprietor, and from his chair, in the center of the room, he presides over the others. And he will not let them forget it. Nothing is more important to him than his power. He exercises it over Nagg and Nell, his parents, by offering to give or withhold biscuits and sugar plums as he commands their attention, participation, or disappearance. Over Clov he holds the power of one who is both master and a sort of foster father. "But for me, . . . no father," Hamm likes to tell him, "But for Hamm, . . . no home" (p. 38).

Evidently Hamm took Clov into the house while Clov was still quite young and raised him to be his servant. He was hardly a generous guardian, however; in fact, he takes pride in having killed any affection Clov might ever have had for him :

> Hamm : You loved me once.
> Clov : Once !
> Hamm : I've made you suffer too much. (*Pause.*) Haven't I?
> Clov : It's not that.
> Hamm (*shocked*) : I haven't made you suffer too much?
> Clov : Yes !
> Hamm (*relieved*) : Ah you gave me a fright !

[pp. 6-7]

As with Nagg and Nell, Hamm uses material possessions as a means of controlling him. When Clov was younger, Hamm had refused him a bicycle, for example : "When there were still bicycles I wept to have one. I crawled at your feet. You told me to go to hell" (p. 8). And now, in a world in which there are no more bicycles to withhold, Hamm tries to torment him with the threat of hunger : "I'll give you just enough to keep you from dying. You'll be hungry all the time" (p. 5). As Clov implies when Hamm orders him to bring him his toy dog, Clov's position is essentially the same as that of the stuffed animal. "Your dogs are here," he says (p. 40). Typically magisterial, Hamm wants to know, "Is he gazing at me? . . . As if he were asking me to take him for a walk? . . . Or as if he were begging me for a bone" (p. 41). "Leave him like that, standing there imploring me," he says.

Clov too, however, is as attached to the relationship as Hamm is. Clov says that he has been trying to leave ever since he "was whelped" (p. 14), but he has never been able to do it. And although he says he cannot understand why he always obeys Hamm, he has obeyed him all his life. As in the relationship of Lucky and Pozzo, it seems the slave needs a master as much as the master needs a slave.

One reason Hamm needs the others is that they serve as a captive audience for his story. It is a story he has been working on for some time. How much of it is fiction, and how much is based on the memory of real events, is not clear. That he calls it his "chronicle" (p. 58) makes it sound at least somewhat historical, but whether the specific events really took place or not, the story is essentially true as a revelation of Hamm's attitudes toward other people and toward life. The scene is a cold, bright winter day, Christmas Eve, and Hamm is putting up decorations. A man comes, "crawling towards me, on his belly" (p. 50), looking for help for himself and his little boy. "Come on, man, speak up," says Hamm. "what is [it] you want from me, I have to put up my holly" (p. 52). When the man asks for bread or corn to revive his boy, Hamm tantalizes him with the description of "a nice pot of porridge . . . a nice pot and a half of porridge, full of nourishment" and of how when the boy eats it the color will "come back into his little cheeks." Then after arousing the man's hopes in this way, he dashes them violently : "Use your head, can't you, use your head, you're on earth, there's no cure for that!" (p. 53). "But what in God's name do you imagine?" he demands, "That the earth will awake in spring? That the rivers and seas will run with fish again? That there's manna in heaven still for imbeciles like you?"

From the context the boy appears to be a symbol of fertility and vitality. He was left "deep in sleep" three full days earlier, recalling the period between the death and resurrection of Christ, whose birth Hamm is preparing to observe, in a purely external way, with holly. Both the birth and the resurrection of Christ are traditional symbols of the renewal of life, but Hamm refuses to contribute to the revival of this present embodiment of the same force. To Hamm life no longer seems worth renewing, even if its renewal were possible. When he later finishes the story, or at least seems to, on page 83, his last words are an unequivocal repudiation of life itself : "He doesn't realize. . . . But you! You ought to know what the earth is like, nowadays. Oh I put him before his responsibilities!"

What is the life that Hamm is rejecting here? And why does he reject it?

It is the life that he and those in his household experience — life as seen through the eyes of this room-skull. The opening speech of Clov presents the whole picture :

Finished, it's finished, nearly finished, it must be nearly finished. (*Pause.*) Grain upon grain, one by one, and one day, suddenly, there's a big heap, a little heap, the impossible heap. (*Pause.*) I can't be punished any more. (*Pause.*) I'll go now to my kitchen, ten feet by ten feet by ten feet, and wait for him to whistle me.

(*Pause.*) Nice dimensions, nice proportions, I'll lean on the table, and look at the wall, and wait for him to whistle me.

[pp. 1-2]

The life these characters know is a slow process of dying. The moments pile up, "grain upon grain," but the impossible culmination always remains somewhere ahead of them. In the meantime, all they can do is comfort themselves with a little order, like the "nice proportions" of the kitchen, and wait impatiently, watching the "light dying" (p. 12) on the walls.

Both outside and inside the house, life is slowly coming to an end. There is "no more nature" (p. 11); in the garden the seeds no longer sprout (p. 13). When Clov looks out the window, he says all "corpsed" (p. 30). The waves are "lead" (p. 31), the sun is "zero," the light is an even gray, "light black. From pole to pole" (p. 32).

Inside, the means of sustaining life, or of making it endurable, are gradually running out. There are no more sugar plums, no more sawdust, no more rugs, no more pain-killers. And far more important, the patterns that gave intelligible structure to life are crumbling. Like Beckett's characters generally, Hamm and Clov are both driven by a need to know. If they cannot know ultimate answers, then they need all the more to feel that the patterns of the details can be grasped, even if the details themselves are trivial. Hamm insists, for example, when Clov talks about leaving, that he will have to have a way of knowing whether Clov has really gone or is "merely dead" (p. 46) in his kitchen. It does not matter that "the result would be the same"; Hamm has to know. To know anything at all, however, is becoming increasingly difficult as the most basic patterns of experience break down.

Clov's description of time as a piling up of moments is an indication of this. The "impossible heap" he hopes for would be both a terminus and a pattern. Hamm, at a later point, takes up the same image: "Moment upon moment, pattering down, like the millet grains of . . . that old Greek, and all life long you wait for that to mount up to a life" (p. 70). The "old Greek" he refers to is evidently Zeno the Eleatic, who is supposed to have used the image of millet grains falling in diminishing quantities — a bushel, a single grain, the ten thousandth part of a grain — in a dispute with Protagoras.[6] Zeno was concerned mainly with the sound of the grains, but Hamm adapts the image to his own purposes as a symbol of the manner in which time seems to be always striving toward a shape, but without ever drawing nearer to it. Once again, as in *Waiting for Godot,* the experience of time echoes that of the Unnamable :

> . . . the question may be asked . . . why time doesn't pass, doesn't pass from you, why it piles up all about you, instant on instant, on all sides, deeper and deeper, thicker and thicker, your time, others' time, the time of the ancient dead and the dead yet un- born, why it buries you grain by grain neither dead nor alive. . . .[7]

Time is a shapeless pile of infernal moments, all alike. "What time is it?" asks Hamm on page four. "The same as usual," answers Clov.

Deprived of natural patterns, Hamm and Clov have to structure their experience by imposing artificial ones on it. Since the even gray light no longer gives them more than vestigial day-night cycles, as though time had slowed down almost to a standstill, Clov has to reconstruct the old pattern by waking Hamm at a certain time and setting him going with stimulants, then at another determined time, preparing him for sleep with a pain-killer. "In the morning they brace you up and in the evening they calm you down," says Hamm, "Unless it's the other way round" (p. 24). And there is another special time to tell stories.

With little real life left, the artificial life created in stories be- comes all the more important. Here is something the characters can still shape, and the way they talk about their technique indicates how important formal control is to them. When Nagg tells his story of the Englishman's trousers, he is depressed to find his technique slipping : "I never told it worse. (*Pause. Gloomy.*) I tell this story worse and worse" (p. 22). Hamm, on the other hand, is still very pleased with his ability; his Christmas Eve story is sprinkled throughout with self-congratulatory asides : "Nicely put that. . . There's English for you. . . . A bit feeble, that. . . . That should do it" (pp. 51-52).

When Hamm is not shaping stories, he makes up various little rituals or games with which to impose pattern on what is left of life in the house. On two occasions, for example, he tries to draw Clov into a "forgive me" game (pp. 7, 12). Clov, however, will not play, as this is probably a game he has long since tired of. Hamm has better luck getting Clove to act out the ritual of asking him to tell his story, though even then he has to do a lot of coaxing:

> Hamm : Ask me where I've got to.
> Clov : Oh, by the way, your story?
> Hamm (*surprised*) : What story? . . . (*angrily*) Keep going, can't
> you, keep going!
> Clov : You've got on with it, I hope.
>
> [pp. 58-59]

And, of course, the play derives its title from Hamm's analogy of his final scene to an endgame in chess: "Old engame lost of old, play and lose and have done with losing" (p. 82).

No matter how rudimentary the form, pattern, to these characters, seems something that must be maintained as far as possible. When Clov wheels Hamm about, for example, for a circuit of the walls or a trip to the window, Hamm is very concerned with returning precisely to the center of the room:

> Hamm : Am I right in the center?
> Clov : I'll measure it.
> Hamm : More or less! More or less!
> Clov (*moving chair slightly*) : There!
> Hamm : I'm more or less in the center?
> Clov : I'd say so.
> Hamm : You'd say so! Put me right in the center! . . . Bang in
> the center!
>
> [pp. 26-27]

Although Clov is not such a gamester or a raconteur as Hamm, he is equally attached to the idea of order and perhaps even more frustrated by its elusiveness. "I love order," he says. "It's my dream. A world where all would be silent and still and each thing in its last place, under the last dust" (p. 57). There is much that is significant in this statement. Clov evidently intends it to mean simply that he would like to attain the final peace of death. But for the audience it suggests far more. It suggests that perfect order of the kind Hamm and Clov long for would necessarily be a kind of death, in the sense that there would no longer be any room in it for movement and change. And it also suggests that perhaps it has been this very attempt to force form on the Protean body of reality that has severed their relationship with the forces of life. Hamm raises several times the question of whether somewhere outside their house, that is, outside the circumscribed world of their present experience, there may still be life. On page 39, for example, he asks, "Did you ever think of one thing? . . . That here we're down in a hole. . . . But beyond the hills? Eh? Perhaps it's still green. Eh? . . . Flora! Pomona! (*Ecstatically.*) Ceres!" Of course his enthusiasm does not carry over into any kind of action. He talks of making a raft and letting the currents carry them south "to other . . . mammals" (p. 34), but when confronted with the reality of such a voyage — "Wait! Will there be sharks, do you think?" (p. 35) — he turns back to his pain-killer.

The possibility that there may be more to the world than the living death Hamm, Clov, Nagg, and Nell see from their point of view in Hamm's house is further suggested by the story Hamm tells of a "madman" he once knew, a painter and engraver :

> I used to go and see him, in the asylum. I'd take him by the hand and drag him to the window. Look! There! All that rising corn! And there! Look! The sails of the herring fleet! All that loveliness! . . . He'd snatch away his hand and go back into his corner. Appalled. All he had seen was ashes. . . . He alone had been spared.
>
> [p. 44]

Even Hamm seems momentarily struck by the possible implications of this. "It appears the case is . . . was not so . . . so unusual," he adds. But again, he does not pursue the idea.

If the vitality of the life in Hamm's household has been diminished by a special way of looking at the world, then it would seem likely that part of the problem derives from an attempt to cling to inadequate ideas and to force them on reality. One reason time has slowed to a stop for both Hamm and Clov is that their clinging to dead ideas will not let it move. "All life long the same questions, the same answers," says Clov (p. 5). For a mind going round and round in the same channel, it is natural that every moment would appear the same. "You've asked me these questions millions of times," says Clov wearily (p. 38). "I love the old questions," answers Hamm, "(*with fervour.*) Ah the old questions, the old answers, there's nothing like them." The familiar, though monotonous, provides a feeling of security.

But it can also become a frustrating trap, and that is what the inhabitants of this house have made of it. Although he holds fast to the old questions and the old answers, Hamm also sees through them, and this leads to boredom and anger. He orders the household to join him in the Lord's Prayer, for example — " Again !" says Clov (p. 54) — but he ends the prayer with a curse : "The bastard! He doesn't exist!" (p. 55). Already beyond the condition of Vladimir, for whom hope in a discredited idea could still be somewhat revived, even if only feebly, Hamm, by his refusal to let go of the old patterns of thought, has chained himself to a corpse.

Another cause of the monotony and barrenness of their existence is the moral isolation that characterizes the life of Hamm's house. "When old Mother Pegg asked you for oil for her lamp and you told her to get out to hell, you knew what was happening then, no?" asks Clov at one point. "You know what she died of, Mother Pegg? Of darkness" (p. 75).[8] Inability to see beyond empty ideas is one form of darkness, but the state of being entirely alone is another, and both can kill. Even when Hamm appears to be reaching out to others in speech, he is not really trying to communicate with them. The only relationship he wants with others is that of a master with dehumanized slaves, and his ham-acting is the opposite of real communication.[9] The performance is mainly for himself; his audience is simply a group of victims for him to impose himself on. Both the separation of the ego from others and the attempt to use old ideas as a shield against reality are aspects of a single moral failure : the attempt to close oneself off from life rather than open oneself to it.

This is Clov's problem as well as Hamm's, of course, but for Clov it is not necessarily the whole story. Hamm predicts, with *"prophetic relish,"* that Clov's end will eventually be the same as his.

> One day you'll be blind, like me. You'll be sitting there, a speck in the void, in the dark, for ever, like me. . . . Yes, one day you'll know what it is, you'll be like me, except that you won't have anyone with you, because you won't have had pity on anyone and because there won't be anyone left to have pity on.
>
> [p. 36]

"It's not certain," answers Clov. And it is not — not only because, as Clov says, he "can't sit down" (p. 37), but also because something is happening.

There are several references during the play to the idea that some kind of change is taking place. On page thirteen, for example, Hamm asks, with anguish, "What's happening, what's happening?", and Clov answers, "Something is taking its course." Then at a later point, after the same exchange, Hamm goes on to ask, "We're not beginning to . . . to . . . mean something?" (p. 32). "Mean something! You and I, mean something!" laughs Clov. It is nothing so comforting as a meaning, however. What eventually happens is something far more surprising: a mystery and a challenge.

The change is taking place not in Hamm, but in Clov. "I was never there," says Hamm, "Absent always. It all happened without me" (p. 74). Hamm has shut himself off altogether from life and change, but in the meantime an obscure process of development has been going on in Clov, and at the end of the play it comes to the surface.

During all their life together Clov has been locked with Hamm in a relationship of hatred and dependence. He would like to kill him, but he never can. He would like to leave, but he never has. "Do this, do that, and I do it. I never refuse. Why?" he asks (p. 43). "You're not able to," says Hamm. Hamm even teases him occasionally with the idea of disobedience: "I can't prevent you," says Hamm when Clov says he wants to sing in spite of Hamm's command not to (p. 73). And Clov does not sing. Hamm has little real power, but Clov has a strong need to obey.

As the end approaches, however, it becomes evident that a new spirit of independence is growing in Clov. Although Clov has been trying all his life to leave and has never succeeded in doing so, it now begins to seem even to Hamm as if perhaps he may. As Clov sets up the alarm clock they had agreed upon as the device that would let Hamm know whether Clov was gone or "merely dead," Hamm asks what he is doing, and Clov answers, "winding up" (p. 72). Hamm then orders him to look at the earth again, "Since it's calling you." And when Clov looks, he sees something completely new and completely unexpected: ". . . a small boy!" (p. 78).[10]

What the sudden appearance of the boy means is as obscure to Clov as it is to Hamm, but what is important is that it starts him thinking in a new way which seems for the first time to be entirely his own. Previously he had always depended on Hamm or at least on others for his categories of thought, and if old categories became inadequate he still looked to Hamm for replacements. When Hamm

taunted him with the meaninglessness of the word "yesterday" in
their world of attenuated time, Clov had answered violently : "That
means that bloody awful day, long ago, before this bloody awful
day. I use the words you taught me. If they don't mean anything
any more, teach me others. Or let me be silent" (pp. 43-44). Now,
however, in trying to understand what this new event means for
him, Clov shifts from dependence on the thoughts of others to a
personal and immediate confrontation with mysterious reality. He
begins by speaking of the ideas that "they" have given to him
throughout his life :

> They said to me, That's love, yes, yes. . . .
> They said to me, That's friendship, yes, yes, no question, you've
> found it. They said to me, Here's the place, stop, raise your head
> and look at all that beauty. That order! They said to me, Come
> now, you're not a brute beast, think upon these things and you'll
> see how all becomes clear. And simple.
>
> [p. 80]

And sometimes, he says, he goes over the same kind of outmoded
processes of thought himself : "I say to myself — sometimes, Clov,
you must learn to suffer better than that if you want them to weary
of punishing you — one day." But now that is behind him : "Then
one day, suddenly, it ends, it changes, I don't understand, it dies, or
it's me, I don't understand that either" (p. 81). There are no concepts for what he now is facing, and he can no longer hide behind
them : "I ask the words that remain — sleeping, waking, morning,
evening. They have nothing to say." Finding "them" silent — collective patterns of thought, the authority of Hamm, all of those
other than himself upon whom he has previously unloaded the
burden of responsibility for his life and acts — he is forced finally
to turn to the obscure forces within his self which are leading him
out of Hamm's house to face what lies beyond : "I open the door of
the cell and go. I am so bowed I only see my feet, if I open my eyes,
and between my legs a little trail of black dust. I say to myself that
the earth is extinguished, though I never saw it lit."

Although there is a new sense of self-reliance evident in this
speech, from Clov's point of view it is hardly a cause for rejoicing.
It is not easy to be one's own man in a universe like this one, so
completely devoid of the signposts that once made it seem familiar,

even if they misled. If Clov really does have the courage to set forth, it is clear neither to him nor to the audience what he will face outside — life, death, or ultimate meaninglessness. Nor is Clov at all optimistic. Although now he says it is easy to go, he also says, "When I fall I'll weep for happiness."

Will he go? The ending is uncertain. Although his new sense of independence enables him to disobey Hamm for the first time — he does not cover Hamm with the sheet when ordered to — and although he changes to traveling clothes, we do not actually see him leave. The stage directions say that *"he halts by the door and stands there, impassive and motionless, his eyes fixed on Hamm, till the end"* (p. 82).

What, then, can we say with certainty about this ending? In Beckett's plays the details of conventional plot are less important than the essential situation, and in this case the essential situation is quite clear, whatever the dénouement. We cannot tell whether Clov will actually leave or not, but what is certain is that he is confronted with the challenge of leaving. The boy who has now appeared in the wilderness, like the boy in Hamm's Christmas Eve story, repre- sents the possibility that life may be renewable, and the new forces stirring within Clov are impelling him toward the exploration of this possibility. Hamm is blind and immobile and has already made his own decision against life; when the boy is sighted Hamm says he is not even worth the bother of killing, though he had previously insisted on Clov's exterminating anything that might serve as a potential progenitor of the human race. "If he exists he'll die there or he'll come here," says Hamm, who now no longer believes that life is even possible : if the boy exists he will die one way or the other, either a physical death in the wilderness or a moral death in Hamm's house. But Clov still has the power to walk out into the world and possibly make a new life of his own. Until now he has lived in Hamm's orbit, seeing the world through Hamm's eyes, which can only see ashes, but if he breaks out of the orbit, as he now seems about to do, his own vision might become an entirely different one. To a person imprisoned within the framework of the "old questions, the old answers" there is no hope for renewal in a world the old patterns of thought cannot fit. Clov, however, is con- fronted with the challenge of learning to walk out into an absurd universe, to face it, and to live in it. Whether this will work out or not Clov does not know, nor do we.

CHAPTER V

Krapp's Last Tape

To follow Clov out into the wilderness would be extremely difficult, and for art perhaps it would not even be possible. Beckett attempts it only once, and in a limited way, in *Cascando*. More often he confines his efforts to what is possible : the study of those who, for one reason or another, have remained behind. Krapp is one of these. As with Hamm, Pozzo, and so many others, the key element in his character is moral isolation. He is a person who, through various choices at different times, has made his life into a prison and who is driven in old age to the realization that he is about to die without having ever really lived. Alone in his room, Krapp looks back on a past that was not lived but avoided. All that is left to him is fragmentary memories, the wreckage of time, bits of debris that remain only to remind him that what is lost is irreparable. What Beckett once said of the characters of Proust is equally true of Krapp, that men

> . . . are victims of this predominating condition and circumstance — Time . . . victims and prisoners. . . . There is no escape from yesterday because yesterday has deformed us, or been deformed by us. . . . We are not merely more weary because of yesterday, we are other, no longer what we were before the calamity of yesterday.[1]

Deforming and being deformed in turn, Krapp has made of his days and years the links of the chains that bind him.

The play begins in silence, Krapp sitting at the table facing the audience.[2] Above the table is a light, around it darkness. His first actions, before any words are spoken, reveal features of his personality that show how closely related he is to many of Beckett's other characters. His first movement, for example, is to consult his watch, evidently an attempt to bring temporal order to the confusion that surrounds him. Then after looking at a note on an envelope, perhaps to check the number of the tape he intends to listen to this evening, he gets out a bundle of keys and begins to unlock, open and close, and relock the drawers of the table, pulling out a reel, not the right one, then a banana. As he takes first that banana, then another in his mouth, he stops, remains motionless, and stares vacuously before him. The keys and locked drawers indicate his attachment to possessions; like Pozzo and so many others, he feels a need to believe that things can be owned and that he can own them. The vacuous stare shows the extent of his absorption in appetite; he is the erotic man reduced to bare essentials. The phallic appearance of the long white banana held protruding from his mouth emphasizes its auto-erotic associations. After removing the second banana from his mouth and putting it into his waistcoat pocket, he suddenly withdraws to the darkness at the back of the stage, takes a drink, as the sound of a cork indicates, then returns with a ledger. He checks in it for the correct number of the tape — box three, spool five — lingers over the sound of "Spooool!" then after some difficulty actually locating it due to the general dis-order among his boxes, he finds it and looks back at the ledger entry to read the summary of its contents.

His reaction is significant. As he reads the notes — mother at rest at last, the black ball, the dark nurse, slight improvement in bowel condition, memorable equinox, farewell to love — he has to stop and puzzle at various entries which refer to elements in his past that he has completely forgotten. His mother he seems to recognize, and his bowel problem — this is still with him, after all, as his later reference to "the iron stool" indicates (p. 25) — but the black ball and the dark nurse have escaped him, as have the memorable equinox and the farewell to love. Even the meaning of the word "equinox" has been forgotten; the Krapp of the present does not even remember the language of the man he once was. It is clear that the tape is going to present Krapp with what Proust called in-voluntary memory, the kind of memory that has special freshness and force when recalled because, having been completely lost to consciousness, it has never had a chance to become dimmed in its outlines by habituation. A memory of this kind brings back not only past events but also the self, quite a different self, that experienced them.

In *The Unnamable* Beckett had presented a picture of the self as a collection of fragmentary thoughts and impulses held together only by certain habits of mind that lead one around and around in already outworn patterns of thought. Here he presents a similar case, a man whose life over a period of some forty to fifty years is seen as a sequence of fragmentary selves held together by habit and by a thread of memory. Once again, Beckett's explanation of Proust, though written twenty-seven years before *Krapp,* can help us to understand his own work :

> Life is habit. Or rather life is a succession of habits, since the individual is a succession of individuals; the world being a projection of the individual's consciousness . . . the pact must be continually renewed. . . . The creation of the world did not take place once and for all time, but takes place every day.[3]

The life a man looks back on is the life of the selves he has made. Though his old selves may be forgotten, his successive patterns of habit grow out of one another, holding him the prisoner of men he can no longer even recognize.

Although Krapp listens to only one tape, that one presents him with three of his former selves, united with each other by certain continuities, principally a continuous egosim, which ironically also isolates them from one another by the mutual lack of sympathy it engenders. Each despises the others. The voice on the tape is that of Krapp as he was thirty years earlier at the age of thirty-nine. It is a stronger voice, and *"rather pompous"* (p. 14). The younger man had just been celebrating his birthday alone at the winehouse and had come home to his "den" and his "old rags," probably the same den he is in now and perhaps the same rags, to listen to an earlier tape and record his present reflections. "Sneers at what he calls his youth and thanks to God that it's over," says the thirty-nine year old Krapp of the earlier one ten or twelve years younger, and then adds, "False ring there" (p. 17). That the pompous ring of his own voice had its own falsity, he did not see, but it is clear to the present Krapp. "Just been listening to that stupid bastard I took myself for thirty years ago," says the present Krapp into his own tape somewhat later — perhaps the "last" tape that the title refers to? — "hard to believe I was ever as bad as that. Thank God that's all done with anyway" (p. 24). The thirty-nine year old Krapp had found it similarly "hard to believe" he was ever "that young whelp" (p. 16) he had been at 27 or 29. Each of them sees through the selves that have gone before, but each remains equally subject to the illusion that anything one has ever done or been can ever be "all done with."

The twenty-seven or twenty-nine year old Krapp had been "living on and off" with a girl named Bianca, who lived in a Kedar Street. "Well out of that, Jesus yes!" says the voice on the tape. "Hopeless business" (p. 16). The younger Krapp had not said much about Bianca, but a reference to her eyes evoked more interest in the thirty-nine year old — "Very warm. I suddenly saw them again. . . . Incomparable!" — than did the younger man's artistic aspirations and resolutions for self-improvement. "What remains of all that misery?" he says, dismissing all the concerns that seemed so important to the younger man, "A girl in a shabby green coat, on a railway-station platform? No?" (p. 17). This is all that remained meaningful to the one on the tape.

For all of his contempt for the seriousness of the younger man, however, the thirty-nine year old was hardly very different. Looking back on his own past year, he tries to separate "the grain from the husks" (p. 14), tries to distinguish, that is, "those things worth having when all the dust has — when all *my* dust has settled" (p. 15). (The correction suggests the exclusiveness of his preoccupation with self.) He lists concerns that strongly resemble those of the younger man and makes similarly lopsided valuations of them. He remembers sitting on a bench alongside a canal watching the window where his mother lay dying "after her long viduity" (p. 18) — a word the present Krapp has to stop to look up — wishing she were dead. Along with this memory come further memories of people he had got to "know" in the vicinity, "oh by appearance of course I mean!" (p. 19), among them the dark nurse to whom the ledger entry had referred. After the blind was rolled down signifying the death of Krapp's mother, a white dog came looking for a black ball he had picked up. Krapp sat for a while contemplating the isolation of all beings within their separate streams of living — "Moments. Her moments, my moments. . . . The dog's moments" (p. 20) — then gave the dog its ball.

None of these memories, however, seemed very important to the thirty-nine year old Krapp, merely random fragments that came back to him by association. What mattered to him was his "vision," evidently an impression of wholeness or purpose transcending and binding together the elements of his life :

Spiritually a year of profound gloom and indigence until that memorable night in March, at the end of the jetty, in the howling wind, never to be forgotten, when suddenly I saw the whole thing. The vision, at last. This I fancy is what I have chiefly to record this evening. . . . What I suddenly saw was this, that the belief I had been going on all my life, namely. . . .

[pp. 20-21]

He is cut off by the present Krapp, who not only has forgotten this vision after all, but is not even interested in it. The present Krapp switches the tape forward, catching another fragment — ". . . clear to me at last that the dark I have always struggled to keep under is in reality my most" — then another, about "the light of the understanding and the fire," until finally he arrives at something more interesting to him, though probably far less important to the Krapp on the tape, a scene in which he was floating in a boat with a girl. "Let that go! Jesus! Take his mind off his homework! Jesus!" says the present Krapp into his own tape later (p. 24), disgusted with his earlier self's priorities. Once again all that is left of value later is a memory like that of the girl in the shabby green coat on the railway platform. But also once again, the new recording begins with a speech which, though delivered in a less vigorous voice, has a similarly pompous, self-important tone: "Everything there, everything on this old muckball, all the light and dark and famine and feasting of . . . the ages!" The difference lies simply in the estimation of what is the famine and what the feasting. "The eyes she had!" he says.

His description of his present activities makes even clearer how little fundamental change there has been, despite his feeling of loss of continuity among his successive selves. He has sold seventeen copies of a book — the "opus magnum" he had dreamed of writing some forty years before? — and spends his time weeping over a book called *Effie*[4] — the same book? — crawling out occasionally to sit shivering in the park and long for death. Sometimes he copulates with a "bony old ghost of a whore" named Fanny. Once he went to Vespers, "like when I was in short pants" (p. 26), but went to sleep and fell off the pew. At night in bed he lies in the dark dreaming of his youth. Disillusioned and tired, he finally gives up after a while on his present tape and turns back to the one of the thirty-nine year old, to the scene in the boat with the girl.

The play ends with Krapp motionlessly staring into space and the tape, come to its send, running on in silence. He has grown to a certain extent through the experience of having to face his past selves — grown, that is, in the sense that he has lost some of his illusion of self-sufficiency and has gained some realization of the loneliness of his life. But this growth has not carried him very far. His self-knowledge is greater than before, but not very deep. He is not healed at the end, but paralyzed.

What went wrong? What choices led him to this dead end? Krapp himself seems to understand very little of this, only that the end he has come to is indeed a dead one. The clues are there, but Krapp is too close to them. The audience, however, is in a position to see more clearly. A pattern of imagery which slowly emerges during the course of the play, the imagery of light and darkness, points toward the answer.

The thirty-nine year old Krapp had said on his tape that he liked the sharply demarcated areas of light and darkness made in his room by the light above the table :

> The new light above my table is a great improvement. With all this darkness round me I feel less alone. (*Pause.*) In a way. (*Pause.*) I love to get up and move about in it, then back here to ... (*hesitates*) ... me. (*Pause.*) Krapp.

> [pp. 14-15]

Evidently light had represented to him consciousness, activity, individuality, the burden of being himself, and the darkness had seemed to him to offer a retreat into the freedom of unawareness. The present Krapp seems to feel the same way. At the beginning of the play when he goes backstage into darkness to have a drink, he moves, according to the stage directions, *"with all the speed he can muster"* (pp. 11-12), as though he were running away from the light, and later when he switches off the tape machine to go have a second drink in the dark, it is as though he were retreating again from another light, the memories that are suddenly coming back to his consciousness.

Of course Krapp probably understands the symbolism of all this — it is he after all who set the light up that way — and it means relatively little. He is not less alone with the dark around him; he only feels that way momentarily. A deeper significance emerges, however, as the association of the ideas symbolized by light and darkness with the various women in his life is gradually revealed. Just as Krapp's life alternates between periods in the light and periods of escape into darkness, so the women in his life represent to him, though he is at best only dimly conscious of it, an ambiguous combination of light and darkness, life and death, challenge and escape. Calling him to adult relationships, they challenge him to become a man, a conscious, fully developed individual with the courage and strength to walk in the light; but at the same time they are a temptation to him to retreat into the relationship of a child with its mother, to the darkness and security of the womb. Either path frightens him : forward into light and a full life, or backward into darkness and spiritual or psychological death. Half in life and half out of it, he can choose neither one direction nor the other. His reactions to the various women he has known have been shaped in large part by this ambivalence.

There is another significance as well in this imagery that is equally relevant to the problem of Krapp's relationships with women and with life. Light, associated as we have seen with consciousness, is an area in which the outlines of things can be seen clearly, sharply delineated and distinct from one another. It corresponds in this sense to rationality, the area of life in which man can conceptualize his experience and therefore feel himself the master of it. Darkness, on the other hand, is associated with the nonrational, the area of mystery, in which man is no longer in control but can only open himself to receive experiences that break down or bypass his concepts, overpower him, and reduce him to submission. In this area, clarity becomes blurred, and consciousness fades off into unconsciousness.

To a person who can see life only rationalistically, only in sharp black and white, as Beckett's characters generally, especially his men, tend to do, darkness is terrifying. To enter into the kind of relationship to which women call him, Krapp would have to accept a life in which the light of reason and the darkness of the nonrational stood side by side, reached out to one another, and interpenetrated. This, however, is something he dreads as though it were a threat to his very being. The irony is that, because he is unable to approach life in this way, that is, to accept it in its full complexity and mysteriousness, he never manages to become fully alive. In the women who come into his life and are driven out of it by his fear, it is not only others who call to him, but his own depths as well.

The first woman mentioned in the play, apart from his mother, is Bianca, whose name, significantly, means white in Italian, and whose setting was Kedar Street. Kedar means "dark" in Hebrew. As a white figure, associated with light, she represented a challenge to Krapp to come to life, to accept the full being of manhood in a relationship with her. At the same time, though, and here the challenge posed special difficulty for Krapp, to be her lover would have meant to accept the darkness of her setting. To be a man in such a relationship would mean to have the courage to live surrounded by mystery. The younger Krapp chose to withdraw from the challenge, and the thirty-nine year old looking back reaffirmed that decision; he felt glad to have escaped. The memory that remained of the relationship was less disturbing than the experience would have been. At a remove of ten or twelve years he was able to forget what drove him away from her and to select from the complex reality, of which she had been a symbol, what was really only one side of her attraction : the warmth of her eyes. Afraid to accept her as a woman, he could reduce her in retrospect to a mother. Looking back from his distance in time he could see that the younger man had failed to realize that Bianca had been more important than his intellectual aspirations, but he had himself forgotten what her true import was. The darkness of her eyes had offered in reality not the warmth of the womb, but the challenge of mystery.

Evidently the only woman with whom Krapp ever had a prolonged relationship was his mother. The thirty-nine year old tells on the tape how he had sat watching her window wanting to be rid of her. As the mother who bore him she must have represented to him the womb that thrust him into the world and the darkness out of which he came. Torn between being and nonbeing, he must have felt resentment against her for having given birth to him and at the same time a fear of the retreat into childlike dependence to which as his mother she continued to be a temptation. Her long state of widowhood — "deep weeds of viduity" (p. 18) — associates her with darkness and withdrawal from life, and the reference the present Krapp finds in the dictionary to the dark plumage of the male vidua bird reminds us, if not him, of the similarity he bears to her. His desire for her death probably grew out of a complicated inner conflict : his resentment, on the one hand, at her having imposed on him the burden of being, and on the other, an equally deep resentment for the paralysis of will in which the temptation she symbolized held him, preventing him from bearing the burden as a man.

This whole complex of attitudes comes together in his reaction to the figure of the "dark nurse."

As an image she combines in her person both darkness and light. The whiteness of her costume suggests the call to conscious being, while at the same time the darkness of her coloring suggests the realm of mystery into which an emotional relationship with a woman would carry him. Her role as a nurse, on the other hand, suggests the possibility of escape into an infantile dependency that would simultaneously deliver him from his manhood and deprive him of it. The thirty-nine year old Krapp's description of her reveals the complexity of his reactions : "One dark young beauty I recollect particularly, all white and starch, incomparable bosom, with a big black hooded perambulator, most funereal thing" (p. 19). The shining bride, with a bosom both sexually enticing and maternal, draws him simultaneously toward manhood and toward infancy, toward activity and passivity, toward life and death.

Her reaction to Krapp is perhaps equally significant. Like the representative of motherhood that she was, at least in part, she threatened to call a policeman when Krapp became "bold enough" to approach her. This may indicate that Krapp's failure to live was not his fault alone. Perhaps it was not only he but the women in his life as well who could not decide whether they were to be wives or mothers to him. Whatever the reason for the loss, however, the sense of loss remains. Looking back at the time of making the tape, he found the image of her eyes still drawing him : "The eyes ! Like . . . chrysolite !"

Some hints of what a fully mature relationship with a woman might have been like if Krapp had been able to live it are provided in the description the thirty-nine year old Krapp gives of the girl in the boat, the scene that the older Krapp finds so fascinating :

I said again I thought it was hopeless and no good going on, and she agreed, without opening her eyes. (*Pause*.) I asked her to look at me and after a few moments — (*pause*) — after a few moments she did, but the eyes just slits, because of the glare. I bent over

her to get them in shadow and they opened. (*Pause. Low.*) Let me
in.

[p. 27]

Here, though he drew away from it even as he approached it, he
seems to have come closer than on any other occasion to a genuine
interpenetration with another person. It is significant that this coming together took place in shadow. To enter into her through her
eyes, the traditional windows of the soul, he had to shield them from
the glare of the sun so that they could open. Similarly, an emotional
sharing of lives can take place only in an area of shadow, not in the
glare of rationalistic conceptualism, but in a condition of openness
to the dark depths of experience.

Perhaps the faint beginnings of an understanding of some of the
complexity of his relationship with the dark side of life embodied
in women was a part of the philosophical vision which seemed so
important to the thirty-nine year old Krapp. His reference to "the
dark" he had always struggled to keep suppressed and to how it
was clear to him at last that this was in reality something very important to him appears to point in that direction. Perhaps he meant
that the emotional nonconceptual side of experience was something
he had not taken sufficiently seriously or had not dealt with adequately. If so, however, it would seem that insight bore no fruit in
action. At the end of that tape he went on to speak of the opportunity for living that was now lost to him, but said that he would rather
think about life than live it : "Perhaps my best years are gone.
When there was a chance of happiness. But I wouldn't want them
back. Not with the fire in me now. No, I wouldn't want them back"
(p. 28). He still preferred "the light of the understanding and the
fire" (p. 21) — the fire of his vision, that is — to the fire of life.

Having made his choice, and having renewed it again and again,
he has arrived at the condition he is now in, old and alone, facing
the approach of the final night to which his Vespers hymn refers,
with nothing to look back on but opportunities rejected and irrevocably lost. His emotional life remains undeveloped and consequently
infantile. Having been afraid to ever get deeply involved with the
emotional side of life, he has never learned how to deal with it
except crudely by either suppressing it altogether — "Last fancies.
(*Vehemently.*) Keep 'em under !" — or by wallowing in it in
sterile, self-centered abandon as he reads his own book, which

whether he realizes it or not, is the story of his own failure to live :

> Scalded the eyes out of me reading *Effie* again, a page a day, with tears again. Effie. . . . Could have been happy with her, up there on the Baltic, and the pines, and the dunes. . . . Could I? . . . And she? . . . Pah !

[p. 25]

CHAPTER VI

Embers

Embers (1959), Beckett's second radio play, continues the exploration of the type of person Krapp represented.[1] The central character in this case, Henry, is a kind of Krapp with wife and child.[2] Since Krapp never allowed himself to become entangled in the life of relationship, we were never given a chance to see what that life would have been like. To a reader or audience with the kind of ethical presuppositions most people have, Krapp's failure to live would seem a failure to live up to an ethical ideal. Normally one tends to associate affirmation of life with ethical good and rejection of it with evil. Consequently one is likely to feel that Krapp "should" have sought happiness with Effie up there on the Baltic among the pines and the dunes. To look at Beckett's plays in this way, however, would be to distort their perspective; it would be to bring to bear on Beckett's world what Hamm called "the old questions" and to reply to these with "the old answers." Krapp is a wretched figure, it is true, both in his prime, at the crest of the wave, as he put it, and in his decline, but there is no special reason to assume that the life to which he said "Pah!" did not deserve precisely that response.

Embers makes clear the ironic ambiguity of this problem. Henry's marriage shows what life demands of those who would live it, and it shows that the life Henry and Krapp reject is pure surface, a kind of veneer on nothing. The life of interaction with others — man and woman; man, woman, and child — may have its claims, but they are not claims that have much to do with value. If Krapp had chosen a life with Effie, with the girl in the boat, with Bianca, or with any of the others who might have offered him the opportunity, he would have been less lonely, as Henry was less lonely when Ada was alive and as he still is when she returns to him in memory, but he would not have been less alone. Company, in the life of the world these men inhabit, is only a distraction from a deep and perhaps inevitable isolation. If there is an ethical failure at all,

77

it would seem rather to be a failure to make a positive choice, to choose either to be or not to be instead of resigning passively to be. Both Krapp and Henry resemble the "trimmers" in Dante's *Inferno,* those who were condemned to wander forever outside the pit of hell because their failure to be either good or evil would give the genuine sinners an occasion for pride.[3] Like these, Krapp and Henry are men who rarely or never rise to the dignity of action. It is largely for want of a more discriminating word that one speaks of their "choices"; choice for both of them is mainly a failure to choose at all. But, perhaps to call even this an ethical failure would be to draw into the picture once again the framework of the old questions and the old answers. Beckett does not ask such questions : he only describes.

The key symbol with which Beckett elucidates Henry's character is the sea. What the sea is in reality is, of course, not what matters; what matters is what it means to Henry. As he sits on the shingles and looks at it, hating, fearing, and drawn toward it, the sea seems to him a symbol of life itself, with the word "life" being understood in its most inclusive sense, the sense in which one uses it when one says that death is a part of life. Henry has spent almost his entire existence on the shore of life, afraid either to leave it or to immerse himself in it. Now, during the time of the play, he sits watching it, looking back on his past and forward toward extinction. As he waits for the death that will come, he tries to drown out the formless roar of the sea with sounds that will distract him from it.

First he tries to summon the memory of his father. Since the memory is not vivid enough to take on a voice of its own, Henry does the talking for both of them. "That sound you hear is the sea," he says, "I mention it because the sound is so strange, so unlike the sound of the sea, that if you didn't see what it was you wouldn't know what it was" (pp. 95-96). Henry's explanation is not there simply for the sake of the radio audience, which might need such a clue just as the dead father would; it is integral to the sea's symbolism. To Henry the vagueness of the sea's roar is a symbol of the formlessness of life. Henry cannot tolerate lack of form any more than the many others among Beckett's characters who try to reduce chaos to order. Henry's way to handle this at the moment is to summon the sound of hooves :

Hooves! (*Pause. Louder.*) Hooves! (*Sound of hooves walking on hard road. They die rapidly away. Pause.*) Again! (*Hooves as before. Pause. Excitedly.*) Train it to mark time! Shoe it with steel and tie it up in the yard, have it stamp all day! . . . A ten ton mammoth back from the dead, shoe it with steel and have it tramp the world down!

[p. 96]

A horse, with shoes of man-made steel that could replace the dull roar of the sea with a sharp, precise beat, would be nature tamed to something man could feel comfortable with. No mammoths from the dead will trample the world down, though; the sounds are there only as long as Henry's imagination can maintain them, and, like his will, his imagination is already beginning to fail. All he has is the increasingly dim memory of his father.

Henry's father is important to him for several reasons. He is both like his father and different from him. Like Mr. Barrel, the station master in *All That Fall,* Henry has inherited his father's world, but unlike Mr. Barrel, he finds himself unable to fill his father's shoes. He has half-willingly, half-reluctantly spent his own lifetime by the sea, the scene of his father's life and death, unable to imitate him in either. His father "loved light" (p. 96) and lived on the sunny side of the bay so that he would have light on the water for his evening swim, but Henry never swims any more and moved long ago to the other side of the bay to be in the shadow. The father's swimming was a symbol both to him and to Henry of his willingness to participate in the life that the human condition offers, with its inevitable limitations and with the ever present possibility of death. It is partially by his feelings of inadequacy at not having been able to follow his father into that life that he is tied now to his father's memory :

You wouldn't know me now, you'd be sorry you ever had me, but you were that already, a washout, that's the last I heard from you, a washout. (*Pause. Imitating father's voice.*) "Are you coming for a dip?" "No." "Come on, come on." "No." Glare, stump to door, turn, glare. "A washout, that's all you are, a washout!" (*Violent slam of door.*) . . . Slam life shut like that! . . . Washout . . . Wish to Christ she had.

[pp. 101-2]

Eventually Henry's father took his dip "once too often" (p. 96), and the question of whether his death was by choice or by accident has evidently haunted Henry ever since. His present evening's meditation is in part an attempt to find the answer.

As is later disclosed in Henry's conversation with the memory or ghost of his wife, Ada, his father's death may have been a suicide precipitated by despair over Henry's failure to participate actively in life. Significantly enough, it took place on a day on which Henry was supposed to have gone bathing with Ada. "You weren't there," says Ada, ". . . I called to fetch you, as arranged. We were to go bathing together." It is characteristic that it would be Ada who was to fetch Henry; it was evidently her drive toward the life of domesticity that drew Henry into marriage and fatherhood, and his reluctance to go swimming with her on that day was a symbolic expression of his reluctance to be drawn into that life. To his family this was a clear sign of just how complete a "washout" he was, and their reaction was disgust and despair :

> None of them knew where you were. Your bed had not been slept in. They were all shouting at one another. Your sister said she would throw herself off the cliff. Your father got up and went out, slamming the door. I left soon afterwards and passed him on the road. He did not see me. He was sitting on a rock looking out to sea. I never forgot his posture.
>
> [pp. 116-17]

The posture had something strange about it, she says, but what it was she could never precisely pin down. What bothers Henry evidently is the question of whether this was merely the posture of a man disgusted with his son or whether it was also that of a man about to drown himself. Ada fades out at this point and Henry has to go on himself to try to reconstruct the remainder of Ada's story, probably a story he has gone over already many times in memory. He imagines her continuing down the path to the tram, taking a seat on the open top, then, suddenly feeling uneasy, getting down again and returning up the path to look for his father and finally, seeing no sign of him, going back down and taking the tram home. The mystery remains unsolved. All Henry can do is go over the story again and again.

If it really was Henry's unwillingness to plunge into life that precipitated his father's death, then his father gave up a bit prematurely. Ada finally did manage to lead Henry to the altar and even to get a daughter out of him. On the other hand, though, his father's estimation of him was essentially correct. For Henry, his marriage was not a wholehearted leap into the waters of life, but only a sort of halfhearted wading in the shallows, and since Ada died, he has returned both figuratively and literally to the shore, where he has remained aloof and estranged from life ever since.

What kind of life was it that Ada led him temporarily into? As Henry looks back on it, it appears a monotonous round of small talk about trivia : "Ada too, conversation with her, that was something, that's what hell will be like, small chat to the babbling of Lethe about the good old days when we wished we were dead. . . . Price of margarine fifty years ago. . . . And now. . . . Price of blue-band now!" (pp. 102-3). The suffocating domesticity of their relationship is revealed as soon as her memory comes to life in his mind and takes voice. "You shouldn't be sitting on the cold stones," she says, "they're bad for your growths" (p. 103), and goes on to ask him if he put on his flannel underwear, irritating him finally to the point where, as though her voice were that of the sea tormenting him again, he calls for the sound of hooves to drown her out. She wants Henry to be involved in life, but never in a way that would violate decorum or convention. This is demonstrated symbolically in the scene in which, after urging him to walk down to the water's edge, she warns him, "Don't wet your good boots" (p. 110). "Don't, don't," says Henry as the memory comes back to him of Ada imploring, "Don't! Don't!", twenty years earlier when Henry, carried away for the moment by the passion she had elicited in him, was seducing her for the first time on the same beach. Ada needed the help of sexual appetite to trap Henry into marriage, but since her goal was respectable convention it is natural that a straightforward copulation in a hollow of the beach would not fit her ideas of propriety. She was always very concerned with what others might think. "Yes," says Henry, "you were always very sensitive to being seen in gallant conversation. The least feather of smoke on the horizon and you adjusted your dress and became immersed in the Manchester Guardian" (p. 113).

It is fitting that their daughter, Addie, was named after her mother, since Ada's whole concern was to make her daughter a slightly more polished version of the kind of genteel conventionality

that was her own goal in life. Now, even after she is dead, she still
has enough power in Henry's memory to impose her will on her
daughter's life through him. It is Ada who insists that Addie must
be taught the accomplishments normally thought proper to a young
lady :

Henry : It was not enough to drag her into the world, now she
          must play the piano.
Ada :   She must learn. She shall learn. That — and riding.

                              [pp. 108-9]

That training Addie for the life that will carry on her mother's
ideals of womanhood — ideals that Ada did not herself embody,
by the way, since she was not taught music and riding until "too
late" and had to suffice with plane and solid geometry — involves
a kind of brutal imposition on nature is made clear by the
paroxysms of wailing from Addie that terminate the imagined piano
and riding lessons. This is what Ada wants, however.

Ada values the life Henry and her daughter distrust, and cannot
understand why it should seem so disturbing. "What's wrong with
it," she asks, referring to the sound of the sea, "it's a lovely peaceful gentle soothing sound, why do you hate it . . . And why life?"
(pp. 112-13). For a while, during their years together, she even
managed to persuade Henry that life might be something he could
live with, and now the memory of that period of engagement in
life stirs in him once again the thought that perhaps life, and its
symbol, the sea, might have been manageable after all : "It took
us a long time to have her. . . . Years we kept hammering away
at it. . . . Listen to it ! . . . It's not so bad when you get out on
it. . . . Perhaps I should have gone into the merchant navy" (p.
114). He even suggests that they go for a row.

Such moments of optimism, however, are fleeting. Most of the
time the sea is a horror to Henry, as when he speaks of its "lips
and claws" (p. 106), or as when, after Ada has spoken of its gentle,
soothing sound, he picks up two large stones and clashes them
wildly together : "Thuds, I want thuds ! Like this ! . . . That's life !
. . . Not this . . . sucking !" (pp. 112-13). As the lips and claws of
the sea suck and tear at the land, so life by a slow, inevitable process of erosion draws Henry into it, if not to live, then eventually to
die. Either outcome is equally frightening to him, and a little bit

shaming as well, since his father had managed to do a more cour-
ageous job of both. It is probably not only the idea of guilt at
having possibly driven his father to suicide that ties Henry to the
memory of his father's last day and to this "old grave" (p. 106), the
sea, but also shame at his inability to imitate his father in that
final decisive act. Ada hints at times that the possibility of suicide
is still open to him, telling him that underneath the surface the sea
is "quiet as the grave. Not a sound. All day, all night, not a sound"
(p. 114) and that if he really wants to "be with" his father, there
would be "no difficulty about that" (p. 115). Such decisiveness
would be beyond Henry, however, and the very suggestion makes
him retreat into a defense he would not normally stoop to, a sense of
conventional propriety : "You seem a little cruder than usual today,
Ada." In fact it is precisely as a defense against thoughts of his own
death that he wants the company of Ada's memory. "Keep on, keep
on !" he implores her when she stops talking, "Keep it going, Ada,
every syllable is a second gained" (p. 117). He means not only that
every syllable is a shaped moment wrested from the formless sea of
time, but also that every moment that he can continue talking to
her delays his return to the story of Bolton and Holloway, a story
into which he projects his own simultaneous longing for and fear
of death.

That the story is only a barely fictionalized picture of his own
life is made clear by Ada's reference at one point to Holloway as
a real person, a physician, who is still alive (p. 112) and by the fact
that as Henry approaches the end of the story he addresses Bolton
in the second person — "the glim shaking in your old fist" (pp.
120-21) — as though he were addressing himself, while Holloway
remains merely "he." Of course the story never actually does reach
an end; for it to end would require the resolution of the problem
in Henry's life that it describes: "I never finished it, I never
finished anything, everything always went on for ever" (p. 97). Ada
remarked on the similarity she sometimes noticed between Henry's
posture and that of his father on the day he died (p. 117), and
Henry probably has spent much of his time thinking of suicide, but
a definite decision for it is quite beyond him. Instead he watches
the fire of his life die slowly, fearing the prolonged death as much
as the quick one, paralyzed in inaction. The story of Bolton and
Holloway presents the whole picture in microcosm.

It begins with Bolton before the fire, "standing there waiting in the dark, no light, only the light of the fire, and no sound of any kind, only the fire, an old man in great trouble" (p. 98). The person he is waiting for is Holloway, to whom he has sent a message that he is in "urgent need" and that Holloway is to bring his black bag. When Holloway comes, he is impatient: "My dear Bolton, it is now past midnight, if you would be good enough . . ." (p. 99). Bolton does not specify what he wants, but his "Please! PLEASE!" indicates that he wants it desperately and that Holloway already knows what it is. Evidently, unable to take action himself to terminate his life, he wants to persuade Holloway to do the job for him. Holloway, who has been over all this before with Bolton, perhaps many times, and who does not want to have "to go through it all again" (p. 120), offers him not the final release he wants, but only the means of enduring life a little longer: " 'If it's an injection you want, Bolton, let down your trousers and I'll give you one, I have a panhysterectomy at nine,' meaning of course the anaesthetic" (as Henry the narrator points out) (p. 119).

A "fine old chap, six foot, burly" (pp. 99-100), Holloway is a man with a firm stance in the world, able to deal with life on the terms it offers. He, like Ada, is willing to accept the human condition, even if this means a life that is shallow and conventional, and his idea of his task as a physician is the preservation of that kind of life, whether this means by the administration of palliatives or whether it requires removing "the whole bag of tricks" as Mr. Tyler called it in *All That Fall* (p. 38). The reminder of *All That Fall* in the reference to the panhysterectomy is significant, since the life Ada and Holloway stand for is essentially the same as that of Boghill, a superficial life that slowly languishes because of the hollowness at its core. The conventional man can endure this kind of life because he can avoid facing its emptiness; a man like Bolton or Henry, on the other hand, who lacks the will and strength to adapt, is deprived of the illusions that adaptation grants to those who choose it, illusions that hide the real emptiness of life behind a screen made up of self-importance, ownership, power, religion, ethical commitment, and so on. Instead, he has to face a meaningless universe in all its raw reality, and to watch helplessly as death slowly and irresistibly creeps over him. The gradual decline of the fire in the grate, with its "dreadful sound" (p. 99) as it falls into embers which glow at first, then slowly grow cold, parallels the process of dying that is going on in Henry, in Bolton, and in the world.

As the story draws toward its end, the fire is out, and a "bitter cold" (p. 119) settles into the room as it has already settled over the "white world" outside. Bolton stands by the window looking through the curtains at the whiteness outside and back to the darkness within, "white, black, white, black" (p. 120), the death within and the death without. Neither Bolton nor Henry can bring the slow erosion to an end, nor can they escape from their consciousness of it. Henry is running out of memories to distract himself with : neither Ada nor his father appears now when he calls for them. And Bolton will end with Henry, and as slowly. Henry looks in his appointment book to see if any other distractions will come to deliver him momentarily from his too acute awareness of the emptiness that lies within him and all about him, and which is slowly extending its dominion over him. A plumber is coming the next morning at nine, but after that, nothing : "Saturday . . . nothing. Sunday . . . Sunday . . . nothing all day. . . . Nothing, all day nothing. . . . All day all night nothing" (p. 121). The play closes as it began, with the sound of the sea.

CHAPTER VII

Two Mimes: *Act Without Words I* and
Act Without Words II

In his two mimes Beckett presents in very simple, stylized form pictures of certain aspects of the human condition. The first of these emphasizes the problem of man's relationship with an external world that is beyond his control and that frustrates all his efforts to make it habitable. The second concentrates on man's relationship with the internal forces that drive him and which, in spite of the fact that they are within him, are equally beyond his control.

Act Without Words I,[1] which was first performed in 1957 on the same program with the initial production of *Endgame,* seems closely related both to that play and to *Waiting for Godot.* In *Godot* the defeat of hope led to the rekindling of the same hope, a vicious circle in which rejected illusions are stubbornly clung to as the only defense against the vision of a meaningless reality. *Endgame* presented the possibility, if not the act, of breaking out of that circle. *Act Without Words I* carries its protagonist, "the man," to a point at which he finally learns the futility of all the hopes the world holds out to him and is able to face this and to resist all temptations to return to them.

The scene is a desert in "dazzling" light. The dry, barren setting is a symbol of the emptiness and inhospitableness of the world man finds himself in, and the dazzling light corresponds to the consciousness man is forced to have of this condition, a consciousness that is both disconcerting and difficult to avoid. It is significant that the man is "flung" onto the stage : Martin Heidegger, a philosopher with whose work Beckett seems to have some familiarity, speaks of *"Geworfenheit,"* the state of being "thrown" or "flung" into existence, as the basic existential situation of man.[2] Man finds himself alive and conscious in a world he did not choose and with various specific limitations in himself over which he has no control. This constitutes what Heidegger calls man's "facticity." The facticity of the man in *Act Without Words I* is that of a person who finds himself thrust into a human condition that makes him thirsty and hot. He does not like the situation, but when a whistle from the wings tempts him to try to leave it, he finds himself flung back into it immediately. When he responds to another whistle from the other side of the stage, the same thing happens again. Already he is beginning to learn not only that he cannot escape from his existence, but also that the world he is compelled to live in is governed by forces that are beyond his control and that like to tease him. Having learned something of this, he ignores the next whistle.

The remainder of the mime is a sequence of further teasing offers and disappointments, and the action is the slow process of learning which finally leads the protagonist to the clear and apparently final realization that to pursue any of the goods the world offers is futile. The man is tempted with various potential delights. A tree descends from the flies, offering him the possibility of shade as a relief from the heat of the sun, and he goes and sits under it. Then as he sits looking at his hands, evidently thinking that his fingernails look as if they need a trim, a large pair of tailor's scissors descend, and the whistle calls his attention to them. He takes them and starts to trim his nails. When the palm fronds close, however, and the shadow disappears, he begins to feel a bit suspicious and therefore drops the scissors and reflects.

Next a small carafe with the label "Water" descends and hovers some three yards above the ground. Unable to reach it from the ground, he is given first one, then another cube in different sizes which he can pile up in order to climb to it. It takes him a while to master the technique, of course — the boxes have to be stacked with the smaller on top of the larger rather than vice versa — and he takes a spill in the process, but finally he succeeds. The process as it works out is interestingly similar to that described by Wolfgang Köhler in *The Mentality of Apes*, which tells of studying the learning processes of apes by dangling bananas high in the air and providing them with sticks to pull them down with or boxes to climb up to them on.[3] The difference between Köhler's experiments and those to which the protagonist of the mime is subjected is, of course, that whereas the apes were at least allowed to enjoy their bananas in peace once they reached them, man is not so fortunate. When our protagonist is about to reach the carafe, it is pulled up a little way to a position just beyond his grasp again. A third cube is offered for another attempt, but when the whistle calls his attention to it, he makes no move, so it is withdrawn. He is learning.

But he learns slowly : when a rope with knots for climbing is let down from the flies, he climbs up it, only to be let fall just as he is about to reach the carafe. His situation is like that of Tantalus in Hades, but the full reality of this becomes clear to him only gradually. He will never be able to receive any substantial benefit from the gratifications that are offered to him, and to pursue them will only lead to greater frustration, but he has to go through quite a number of attempts before he can realize how futile they are. And there is no way that he can revenge himself on his situation or escape from it. He makes the mistake of trying to cut the rope with the scissors, perhaps in an attempt at revenge, but then is pulled into the air so that when he cuts it he falls again. With the length of rope that remains, he tries to lasso the carafe, but this is immediately pulled out of sight. Then he thinks of hanging himself from the bough of the tree, but is defeated when the bough droops. Having learned something from this, he renounces the rope and the boxes he was going to use to climb up to the bough, but forgetting one of the earlier lessons he lets himself be tempted to try to walk off stage again when he hears another whistle from the wings. Of course this attempt is no more successful than the others : ne is "flung" back onto the stage, taking a spill as usual. He resists the next whistle, from the other side of the stage, but makes the mistake of thinking once again that perhaps he might be able to escape by suicide. Taking up the scissors to trim his nails, he notices the sharp edges they have and opens his collar to cut his throat. Just as he is ready to do it, of course, the scissors disappear. He sits down on the large cube to reflect on all of this, but this too proves to be a mistake : the cube is pulled out from under him and then up into the flies.

Now he is left alone except for the tree. Having fallen to the ground when the cube was pulled away, he makes no effort to rise this time, but lies there, his face toward the audience. The carafe is lowered again, and the whistle tries to entice him to look at it, but this time he ignores it. The carafe dangles and moves about in front of his face, but still he takes no notice of it, and it is removed. The bough of the tree returns to its horizontal position, and the palm fronds open to bring back the shade, but when the whistle tries to tempt him to move over to it, he remains where he is. Finally the tree is removed and he is left completely alone looking at his hands. What he thinks as he looks at them we cannot know. It could be something like, "What can I do with such a situation?", or it could be, "Now I shall have to rely on myself." It could also be a little of both. At any rate, he has come to an understanding of his situation. He sees that he can rely on nothing outside himself, and is determined not to be seduced again away from this realization.

Act Without Words II (1959) explores the internal dimension of man. If man cannot rely on anything outside himself, is there anything inside him which might prove more worthy of his hope and trust? What *Act Without Words II* has to say about this is that man is driven by a compulsive force that will never let him withdraw for long into inaction. This is an idea that was previously set forth in elaborate detail in the trilogy.[4] Here it is presented in simple form in the life patterns of two men, A and B. Like Vladimir and Estragon, A and B are two very different types who, taken together, present a composite picture of man. A is "slow, awkward," and "absent." Unlike the brisk, businesslike B, he has little real interest in this world, preferring to place his hopes in another, as his praying at the beginning and end of his sequences indicates. The action begins with the arrival of the goad, representing man's inner compulsion to activity. The goad goes to the sack in which A sleeps and pokes it to waken him. A's reluctance to begin his daily round is suggested by the fact that the goad has to poke twice to rouse him.

A's day is not a long one, nor is it enthusiastic. He crawls out of his sack, broods, prays, broods, and so on, stopping after each of his activities to brood a few moments before going on to the next. He puts on the clothes which he shares with B and which B had evidently tended very carefully, since they are folded in a neat pile by B's sack. He starts to eat a bite of carrot, but spits it out in disgust, then carries his and B's sacks to the middle of the stage, broods, takes off the clothes, letting them fall into an untidy heap, broods, prays, and finally crawls back into his sack. Evidently carrying the sacks to a new position is his appointed task, and once he has done it he can go back to sleep.

The goad returns, this time poking B awake. B only requires one poke and is much more enthusiastic about his day than was A. Everything he does, he does vigorously. Where A brooded between activities, B consults his watch, eleven times in all, or his compass and map. Evidently he is the type who likes to orient himself precisely in space and time. He dresses rapidly and carefully. His bite of carrot he "chews and swallows with appetite." He does not bother to pray; evidently he finds this world quite absorbing enough and is confident of his ability to deal with it. After performing his own duty by carrying the sacks to the further side of the stage, he removes the clothes A had left in an untidy pile and folds them neatly once again, winds his watch and crawls back into his sack.

The goad returns, goes over to A's sack and pokes. No response. After another poke the sack begins to move and A crawls out, stops, broods, and prays. The round is ready to begin again. The impression we are left with is that this cycle of arousal, activity, and return to rest has been going on since the beginning of time and will continue forever, if not in the persons of A and B then in those of others who will replace them and be substantially identical with them. The world man is thrown into may be absurd, and the progress man works toward may be as meaningless as the endlessly repeated shifting of the positions of sacks, but he has no choice about living in and for it. The conditions that govern him, both within and without, see to that.

CHAPTER VIII

Happy Days

Act Without Words II represented man as governed by compulsions over which he had no control. The question of whether or not he might be able to free himself from these and direct the course of his energies autonomously was not brought up. The characters were portrayed from the outside and very simply; we saw only that when the goad set them in motion they moved. Beckett's next play, *Happy Days*, carries the exploration of this aspect of man's life a good deal further, showing what goes on inside the mind of a person subject to compulsive control of this kind.[1] And, though it does not present an answer, it does raise the important question that the mime did not.

The basic situation is once again that of a person thrown into a condition with frustrating limitations and with the choice of either facing this directly and clearly or evading it. The central character in this case is Winnie, a rather full-blown, blond woman of about fifty, who is buried to above her waist in the center of a mound. Since Willie, her husband, rarely speaks or shows himself, he is largely peripheral to the play and is present primarily as an object of relationship for Winnie. All one sees of the earth is covered by scorched grass. On the backcloth an unbroken plain and sky recede to meet in the distance. The design of the set, with its *"maximum of simplicity and symmetry"* (p. 7), carries our eyes to the center of attention, Winnie. The fact that she is buried in the earth is a symbol both of the way the absurd is closing in on her as death approaches, making it harder and harder for her to find distractions from herself, and also of the way she has given up her freedom to objects outside her by burying herself in that which is not herself. That the mound has not only been imposed on her by life but is also something she has chosen for herself is made clear by the reference to her feeling of having "to cling on" (p. 34) so as not to float up out of it.

The action begins when a piercing bell rings to awaken her. It has the same kind of difficulty rousing her that the goad had with A; it has to ring twice, first for ten seconds, then for five, before it finally gets through to her. Evidently she would prefer to remain asleep — in fact she says a little later that Willie's faculty for sleeping most of the time is a "marvellous gift" (p. 10) and that she wishes she had it — but nevertheless when she finally wakes, her first effort is to muster up her courage and look at life cheerfully : "Another heavenly day" (p. 8). Her next act is to pray in the traditional way — "For Jesus Christ sake Amen" — before commanding herself to "begin" her "day."

The fact that Winnie wants to make her experience a "day" is significant. Man cannot live without order, and in a world without a time scheme he will impose a pattern of his own making. There are no more days now, and when she is not busy making them up she knows this. "The old style," she says at one point when she sees the label on her medicine bottle telling her to take six level tablespoons "daily" (p. 13). "All day long" in the world she lives in now means only "between the bell for waking and the bell for sleep" (p. 21), but she likes the "old style" the way Hamm liked the "old questions" and the "old answers" and does her best to retain what she can of it in her "daily" life.

In structuring her day she tries to give it, like an Aristotelian plot, a beginning, middle, and end. There has to be a time for brushing her teeth, which comes at the beginning, for rummaging among her things, for singing her song, which should come sometime near the end, and finally for going back to sleep when the bell rings. The trouble, of course, is that never knowing when the bell will ring to signal the end, she can never be certain the middle is being adequately arranged : "To sing too soon is fatal, I always find. . . . On the other hand it is possible to leave it too late. . . . The bell goes for sleep and one has not sung" (p. 56). Anxieties of this kind are something of a blessing for her, however; they distract her from the situation as it really is : a formless chaos on which patterns can be fitted only by self-deception.

Another important distraction, as well as a deep compulsion, is the need she has to know. The object of knowledge is not important; it need not be anything particularly significant. All that is required is that the search for it keep her mind occupied. There is her toothbrush, for example. When she finishes brushing her teeth, she looks at the handle of the brush and tries to make out the writ-

ing on it : ". . . genuine . . . pure . . . what?" (p. 10). She polishes
her spectacles and tries again, then gets a magnifying glass out of
her bag and finally manages to decipher it : "Fully guaranteed . . .
genuine pure . . . hog's . . . setae" (pp. 17-18). Every now and then,
as in this instance, such a quest for knowledge brings her up against
a reminder of the emptiness and sterility of this world in which
"nothing grows" (p. 47). In this case, inquiring from Willie the
difference between a hog and a swine, she finds that a hog is a
"castrated male swine. . . . Reared for slaughter" (p. 47). She manages, however, to avoid thinking about the associations that go with
this, the parallel to her own situation and to Willie's, by shifting her
attention to her joy in the fact that Willie has finally spoken to
her : "Oh this *is* a happy day!" Another object of curiosity, with
similarly unpleasant associations for her, is a pornographic picture
Willie shows her when she asks if she can see it. "No but this is just
genuine pure filth," she exclaims as she examines it intently. "Make
any nice-minded person want to vomit" (p. 19). Then she gets her
magnifying glass to give it a better look : "What does that creature
in the background think he's doing? (*Looks closer.*) Oh no really!"
Finally she gives it a "last long look" before returning it with a
"Pah! . . . Take it away!" No source of curiosity is too trivial or
too repulsive to defeat her. She is always grateful for something —
whether the hairs of the head are called "it" or "them" (p. 22),
how the comb and brush got back into her bag if she did not put
them there — that can keep her mind occupied and diverted from
the real unpleasantness of her life.

And when these distractions fail her, when she loses heart and
envies the brute beast, as she says, she turns to thoughts of death,
either the death that will come, she hopes, with the end of the
world — "the happy day to come when flesh melts at so many
degrees and the night of the moon has so many hundred hours"
(p. 18) — or suicide. Of course, as might be expected, her feelings
about death are as equivocal as those of any of Beckett's other characters. This is made clear by her reaction to her revolver when she
runs across it while rummaging in her bag : she brings it out, holds
it up, "kisses it rapidly," then puts it back (p. 13). She calls it by a
pet name, "Brownie," and likes to know that it is there, but the
sight of it makes her uncomfortable. Death is a pleasant fantasy as
long as it remains at some remove, but when it comes too close it is
as disturbing as reality itself.

The most important of her defenses is talk. Like Vladimir and Estragon, she talks so that she will not have to think, and what she is most afraid of is the possibility that there may come a time when she will no longer be able to talk, either because words will fail her —"Words fail, there are times when even they fail" (p. 24) — or because there will be nobody left to talk to. If it were simply words that failed she would still be able to occupy herself with her possessions, and consequently she is careful not to "overdo the bag" (p. 32) lest she exhaust its interest before the time when she will really need it. But if she were to lose Willie so that she were left entirely alone, she would have to face the emptiness that would be left in her by the absence of the other whose perception of her she had relied on to constitute her personality. The thought of no longer having an interlocutor to direct herself toward is especially abhorrent to her : "Oh no doubt the time will come when before I can utter a word I must make sure you heard the one that went before and then no doubt another come another time when I must learn to talk to myself a thing I could never bear to do such wilderness" (p. 27). Since what Winnie knows of her being is largely confined to that which is reflected in the eyes of others, to be deprived of those eyes, or ears, would be something more frightening to her than death itself.

Sometimes she feels a need to imagine some perceiver other than Willie, perhaps because Willie perceives her mainly through his ears, which leaves her without eyes to round her out : "Strange feeling that someone is looking at me. I am clear, then dim again, then clear again, and so on, back and forth, in and out of someone's eye" (p. 40).

Vladimir, in *Godot,* had had a similar feeling at the point at which he came face to face with the vision of cyclical time, and perhaps his feeling originated in a similar need for defense against the full realization of the aloneness in the depths of man's being : "At me too someone is looking, of me too someone is saying, He is sleeping, he knows nothing, let him sleep on."[2] Or perhaps in both of these cases there is also a feeling of growing awareness of potential self-perception as Winnie and Vladimir become dimly aware of their own reality. If so, then Winnie's awareness is hesitant and unclear, and Vladimir's involves a choice of not waking up, that is, a choice of going on imagining that he is waiting for a Godot who means something. It is also quite possible that both meanings are simultaneously present in their minds. Beckett's man is nothing if not complex.

If Winnie's intimations of eyes watching her have both implications, it is nevertheless clear which she chooses to attend to. After becoming anxious about the possibility of falling into silence, then looking around for something to do and turning finally to filing her nails, she imagines a story, or recalls a memory, in which the eyes are comfortably removed to a distance, that is, located outside herself in other people : "There floats up — into my thoughts — a Mr Shower — a Mr and perhaps a Mrs Shower. . . . Well anyway — this man Shower — or Cooker — no matter — and the woman . . . standing there gaping at me" (pp. 41-42). And as she tells the story she continues filing her nails, as though she were concerned with how she would look to the people she has imagined : "Shower — Shower. (*Inspects filed nails.*) Bit more like it. . . . Keep yourself nice, Winnie, that's what I always say, come what may, keep yourself nice. (*Pause. Resumes filing.*) Yes — Shower — Shower" (p. 41).

In this way and in others, art is one of Winnie's more important defenses. Like the narrator of Eliot's *The Waste Land,* Winnie draws on the entire cultural tradition of western man for fragments to shore against her ruins. Her language throughout the play is sprinkled with quotations or misquotations from such authors as Shakespeare, Milton, Herrick, Gray, Keats, Browning, and, as the play moves along, cutting her off more and more from everything of real value, from a variety of increasingly minor poets.[3] As she says toward the end when she has difficulty remembering the precise wording of one of her tags, "One loses one's classics," the classic in this case being "those exquisite lines. . . . Go forget me why should something o'er that something shadow fling . . ." (p. 57). But even when the tags are at their freshest, she cannot eliminate from them the traces of unhappiness and disappointment they bring with them from the world out of which they grow, as in the first that she introduces : ". . . woe woe is me . . . to see what I see" (p. 10), a slightly distorted recollection of the words of Ophelia on leaving Hamlet after she has had to witness his feigned madness (*Hamlet,* Act 3, scene 1). Or as in the line, "Oh fleeting joys . . . oh something lasting woe" (p. 14), a version of Milton's "Oh fleeting joys/Of Paradise, dear bought with lasting woes !" (from *Paradise Lost,* book 10, lines 741-42).

Nor is music an entirely satisfactory escape. Music actually does cheer her up a bit when she can enjoy it, or it would seem to since she smiles on the occasions when she hears, hums, or sings the "Merry Widow Waltz," but the cheer it provides is short-lived, letting her lapse back into ordinary reality as soon as it ends and the lingering memory of it fades. This is why she speaks of "the sadness after song" to Willie near the end. "Sadness after intimate sexual intercourse one is familiar with," she says, after all Aristotle pointed that out, but the sadness after song is also something that life forces her to recognize. Perhaps the reason music is, of all the escapes she has, the one that seems to be the most successful, even if only momentarily, in allowing her to forget unhappines is that it is a pattern that is purely artificial — not an attempt to impose pattern on a reality that has none, but a genuine escape into an imaginary realm in which there is no need to deceive oneself into believing that imagination and reality are the same. In ordinary reality Winnie has to wrestle with the stubborn insistence of the real in order to try to fit it into the strait jacket of meaning. This produces the kind of anxiety Watt felt when he found that he could no longer fit his concept "pot" onto Mr. Knott's pots. When art can escape from meaning, something music does more successfully than literature, it can succeed in sidestepping the issue.

But not for long. No song can alter or permanently obscure the inescapable reality of Winnie's situation : buried in the scorched earth, in the blazing sun that never sets, waking and sleeping at the command of a force that manipulates her like a puppet. In all of this she persists in her attempt to avert her face, affirming over and over against all obstacles that "this *is* a happy day, this will have been another happy day!" (p. 64). It is not. The reality she will not look at is that it is neither "happy" nor a "day."

Does this steadfast refusal on Winnie's part to face reality mean, then, that her story is purely static, that she does not go through any kind of growth during the play? Not at all. Her life brings her closer to the vision she seeks to avoid even if it does so against her will. Reality presses upon her, both from the outside and from within. Even if it does not break through to her during the course of the play, we can see the direction in which things are moving.

The pattern of her conflict with the reality that is forcing itself upon her can be seen very clearly in the episode of the parasol. She holds up the parasol as a protection against the heat and light of the sun, just as she affirms the illusion of the "happy day" against the threatening vision that would destroy "the sweet old style" (p. 22) of traditional concepts. Then at one point, just as she is expressing gratitude to her imagined God for "great mercies" (p. 37), the parasol bursts into flame : something has happened that is absurd, that is, something has happened that can no longer be explained in terms of "the sweet old style" of natural laws in which every event is linked to every other in a reassuringly tidy sequence. The absurd is there in front of her and threatens to break through her defenses. Her immediate reaction is to turn to the defenses and attempt to bolster them : "I presume this has occurred before, though I cannot recall it. . . . Can you, Willie?" She tries to maintain the rational façade she has imposed on the universe by assimilating this extraordinary event to the pattern of the ordinary, and since this is not easy for her to do by herself, she tries to get help from Willie. As usual, he is not much help. He signals his presence, but does nothing to confirm her in her attempt to reduce the inexplicable to explanation. Consequently she must push on by herself; she has to admit that this never did happen before, but she still tries to explain it in terms that will make it seem not so surprising : "With the sun blazing so much fiercer down, and hourly fiercer, is it not natural things should go on fire never known to do so, in this way I mean, spontaneous like" (p. 38). From this idea she drifts off into others about the eventual arrival of her own death by way of the same natural process, about her gradual burial in the mound, and so on, trying occasionally to elicit or imagine a response from Willie. This leads her into further difficulty, however. The mound, after all, is as mysterious as the igniting of the parasol, and this process of thought brings her around again to the inevitable fact that there is much in her world that is irreducibly mysterious :

> Yes, something seems to have occurred, something has seemed to occur, and nothing has occurred, nothing at all, you are quite right, Willie. . . . The sunshade will be there again tomorrow, beside me on this mound, to help me through the day. (*Pause. She takes up mirror.*) I take up this little glass, I shiver it on a stone — (*does so*) — I throw it away . . . it will be in the bag again tomorrow, without a scratch, to help me through the day. . . . No, one can do nothing. . . . That is what I find so wonderful, the way things . . . (*voice breaks, head down*) . . . things . . . so wonderful.

[p. 39]

D

As she falters here, she is almost driven to look absurdity in the face. Almost, that is, but not quite. What happens next is that she fumbles anxiously in her bag, finally bringing out the music box and escaping through it into art.

This is not the end, however, of the effect of this episode. Her reluctant realization that in the igniting of the parasol a something that was nothing had occurred lingers in the back of her mind and seems to contribute something of its own to the story of Mr. and Mrs. Shower — or Cooker — that she brings up soon afterwards. In its way, this story is far more than just the sort of escape into memory or fantasy that she intends it to be, it is also a kind of commentary by a deeper level of her own mind on the real significance of the parasol incident. As the man and woman stand "gaping" at Winnie in the story, the man asks what Winnie is doing there : "What's she doing? he says — What's the idea? he says — stuck up to her diddies in the bleeding ground — coarse fellow — What does it mean? he says — What's it meant to mean? — and so on — lot more stuff like that — usual drivel" (pp. 42-43). The man's questions are, of course, precisely those that Winnie asks of herself about everything in her life; man must find meaning, whether there is any in reality or not, and Winnie and the man in her story share in this need. The woman's reply, on the other hand, puts into words another aspect of Winnie's attitude toward her world, the realization that is growing deep within her that meaning and reality have no relationship : "And you, she says, what's the idea of you, she says, what are you meant to mean? It is because you're still on your two flat feet, with your old ditty full of tinned muck and changes of underwear. . . ." It is because of this, she means, because he is still firmly planted in the conventional life that shields him from meaninglessness that he can think such questions as he is asking have answers. The fact that Winnie recalls or invents such a story reflects a growing, though strongly resisted, awareness in Winnie that it is absurd to ask what the absurd is meant to mean.

Act II carries this process of growth still further, even if not to completion. Whereas Winnie opened and closed the first act with conventional prayers and tried to persuade herself that they would be effective in bringing her relief from her misfortunes — "prayers perhaps not for naught," she says at one point on thinking of how sometimes her headaches go away (p. 12) — the second act opens without petitionary prayer, but only with "Hail, holy light" and an attempt to believe that "someone is looking at me still" (p. 49). Of course the "someone" is still the God of "the sweet old style," and the greeting to the "holy light" is a quotation from Milton's invocation to the uncreated light of God, but the fact that she is not explicitly praying for something to be given her would seem to indicate some growth in self-reliance. "I used to pray," she says, "I say I used to pray. . . . Yes, I must confess I did. (*Smile.*) Not now" (p. 50).

The reason she smiles as she says this is probably that she feels some degree of liberation in being able to get along without prayer. Her smile does not last, however; freedom may have its pleasant side, but it is also rather frightening. She stops to reflect that if this indicates a change in her, it is not clear what kind of change is involved and that perhaps it may be leading toward more change than she wants: "Then . . . now . . . what difficulties here, for the mind. (*Pause.*) To have been always what I am — and so changed from what I was" (pp. 50-51). She goes on both to introduce and avoid the idea that something might be happening inside her that ~~up that seem to close in peace . . . to see . . . in peace. (Pause.) Not~~ could eventually lead to a radical break with her past: "Eyes float up that seem to close in peace . . . to see . . . in peace. (*Pause.*) Not mine. (*Smile.*) Not now." The eyes she feels floating up inside her would seem to be the eyes of a new vision that would enable her to look on the reality of her world without anxiety over its lack of meaning. She does not want them yet, though: the "old style" is still too precious to her. She turns aside from these thoughts to return to the old question and answer game, to concern with her appearance, and to the last of her possessions, the gun. Even this flight from what is happening, however, leads her inescapably back to the heart of the problem. Thinking about her things, she is forced to face for a moment the fact that like all the rest of reality they are not hers: they are only what they are. Possession is an artificial meaning imposed on an indifferent reality by man's imagination: "It's things, Willie. . . . In the bag, outside the bag. . . . Ah yes, things have their life, that is what I always say, *things* have a life. . . . Take my looking-glass, it doesn't need me" (p. 54). Things have a life of their own; they do not need her or any other person. Of course this is not what she "always" says — quite the contrary — but this thought, like so many others, feels

more comfortable to her when she can take the edge off its new-
ness by persuading herself that it is not unfamiliar.

These thoughts in turn lead to reflections on the role of the bell
in her life, raising the question of the possibility of autonomy :

> The bell. . . . It hurts like a knife. . . . A gouge. . . . One cannot
> ignore it. . . . How often . . . I say how often I have said, Ignore
> it, Winnie, ignore the bell, pay no heed, just sleep and wake,
> sleep and wake, as you please, open and close the eyes as you
> please. . . . But no. (*Smile.*) Not now. (*Smile broader.*) No no.

Perhaps the new life that would emerge from the new vision that
seems to be growing inside her would involve both freedom from
the need to impose artificial patterns on a reality they do not fit
and freedom to direct her own acts with her own will, no longer
submitting to the authority of the bell any more than to that of
the God she imagines or to that of the possessions which in fact
possess her. This is not something she can accept, however. Freedom
is no more endurable to her than meaninglessness.

She retreats into a story. Still, this turns out to be no more satisfactory an escape than any other. All roads lead to the same end :
defeat. In this case the story is a thinly veiled projection of her
own life into fiction. It is about a little girl named Mildred or Millie
who has a doll with "china blue eyes that open and shut" (p. 55),
like Winnie's, and a "pearly necklet," like that Winnie wears. Millie
decides "to undress Dolly," rather the way the new self in Winnie
represented by the eyes floating up from her depths is undressing
Winnie by stripping from her all the conventional ideas that shield
her from naked contact with the hard light of reality. Then suddenly a mouse appears in the story, disturbing Winnie sufficiently
to make her discontinue it for a while. Evidently the mouse is a symbol to her of the destructive element she feels threatened by in the
process of change she is undergoing. When she returns to the story
later, she describes the mouse running up Millie's "little thigh" (p.
59). And as the little girl begins to scream in the story, Winnie gives
a *"sudden piercing scream"* of her own, an indication of how closely
she identifies with her protagonist. When the parents come, she says,
it is "too late." Evidently Winnie feels the same of her own case :
that the undressing that is taking place in her will lead to the
destruction not only of her superficial identity, the self that lives

in conventional ideas and in the eyes of others, but also of the deeper self within. She cannot believe that the loss of all her normal patterns of thought and behaviour would not destroy her very being as well.

At the end she retreats as usual to what she believes is the safer ground of her fortress of illusions, to the old dream of her "happy day." It does not seem likely, however, that this fortress will be able to stand indefinitely. The signs of change are too great. It is hard to tell just what it means when Willie appears, for the first time, dressed up in morning clothes, complete with top hat and white gloves, and tries without success to crawl up the mound to reach her. The attire suggests that the occasion is one of some solemnity, perhaps a death, though just what kind of death is not clear. Winnie makes of it what she must, a sign that this "will have been a happy day, after all, another happy day" (p. 62), and when Willie gasps her name, she rejoices and makes of it another occasion for flight into song. We already know of the sadness that comes after song, however, and we know how fragile the illusion of the "happy day" is. All we can be certain of about this ending is that Winnie will not find in it the meaning she expects. It would seem more likely that the process of change we have seen working itself out in her will lead her to an end she cannot imagine and into which we cannot follow her.

CHAPTER IX

Words and Music

Words and Music (1962), a radio play, is an allegory of art as a process of imaginative exploration.[1] What it explores is the situation of the artist in relation to his life; that is, it attempts to embody in artistic form, in a fusion of emotion and rational thought, an adequate vision of the artist's reality. This, of course, is the very vision that was urging itself so oppressively on Winnie in *Happy Days* and that she tried so anxiously to avoid. In this case, however, the vision is not pressing itself on the central character, but rather seems difficult to attain; consequently it seems not so much a threat as a good to be striven for. In Beckett's characters generally, there is a fundamental ambivalence toward reality, just as toward life and death. When life seems too much with them, they long for death, and when death comes too near, they withdraw from it in horror. Similarly, a thirst for being draws them toward the vision of the real when it seems remote, and a fear of the lonely individuality of actual existence makes them flee from reality whenever it comes to seem too definite. For the artist in *Words and Music* reality still has appeal, perhaps because he is not being forced to face it directly but can pursue it indirectly in the distancing medium of fiction. The goal, however, is the same as that which alternately oppressed and enticed the earlier characters of Beckett's plays : the truth of his life.

The play depicts dramatically the creation of such a vision. Three forces are involved : Croak, Words, and Music. Croak is the name the dialogue directions give to the conscious self of the artist. It is he who sets the other forces in motion by his command and watches them critically as they work, holding them on course, recalling them to it when they stray, or silencing one or the other when an impasse has been reached or when reflection is needed before proceeding further. Music, besides representing the art of music in the simple sense, also symbolizes the element of nonrational feeling that enters into the process of creation and that serves as in many ways a surer, though less articulate, guide than reason to the personal reality of one's life. Words corresponds to the articulate and rational element in this process — and in human nature generally — which has greater difficulty than Music in entering the areas the artist wishes to explore, but which is nevertheless necessary if the experience of reality is to be expressed objectively in full clarity. Of course, to make too precise a distinction between thought and feeling would be to oversimplify; in fact, there is no thought without some element of feeling associated with it, nor any feeling that does not involve some cognitive content. In this case, however, they tend from the point of view of Croak to be all too separate and partial, and what he desires is to bring them together into a unity that will be not only their completion, but his as well.

The play begins with Words and Music alone in the dark. Without Croak they can continue to exist, but only in a rather shadowy way. They have a kind of latent life of their own in the artist's unconscious, but without his conscious direction their energies remain uncoordinated : Words can ruminate over old ideas, and Music can tune up, but neither can move forward alone. So, when the play opens, before Croak arrives to begin the evening's composition, we hear Words trying to silence Music — "Please!" (*Tuning dies away.*) How much longer cooped up here, in the dark? (*With loathing.*) With you!" (p. 23) — so that he may turn to his own activity, a rather mechanical rumination on sloth. The fact that this meditation of his is *"rattled off"* in a low voice as though he were reciting makes it clear that it is not original thinking but rather a mulling over of long familiar material. What he says about sloth is in fact a pretty standard description, the kind of analysis with which traditions of moral philosophy are replete. Left to its own devices, thought has no interest in exploring new territory but prefers to occupy itself with comfortable old clichés.

Croak shuffles in to put an end to this and to marshal Words and Music for real activity. He addresses them by name — Joe for Words, Bob for Music — as though to emphasize that although he is the one who calls them to attention and directs their energies, and although they are really a part of his own larger self, they have a certain degree of independence from him : he cannot get along without their cooperation any more than they can without his. "My comforts!" he says, "Be friends!" This is simultaneously a command to them to work in harmony with each other and a sort of invocation asking them, his muses, to be friends with him. He then asks their forgiveness for his delay, muttering broken phrases that suggest he was delayed on the stairs by the vision of a face. It is this preoccupation with a face that establishes the theme for tonight's session : love.

Croak orders Words to begin, and when Words hesitates — this is evidently not a subject that particularly appeals to him — Croak reinforces his command by thumping his club on the ground. In an *"orotund"* voice, as though commencing a formal declamation, Words simply repeats the formula he had used earlier to describe sloth, even slipping into using that word again so that he has to stop and correct himself : "Of all these movements then and who can number them and they are legion sloth is the LOVE is the most urgent and indeed . . ." (p. 24). The groans of Croak during this recitation show how unsatisfying he finds such formulae. Finally he shuts off Words with a violent thump of his club and orders Music to try to express the theme of love musically. Music makes a stab in this direction, drowning out the protestations of Words, who probably not only wants the limelight to himself but also distrusts the kind of nondiscursive knowledge that Music represents. Evidently Music is better able to enter this new territory than is Words.

Nevertheless, difficult as it may be, verbal articulation is also necessary, and therefore Croak turns back to Words, trying to win him over — "Joe sweet" (p. 25) — and to persuade him to push ahead. This puts Words in an awkward position, since he has come to the end of the prepared formula and will now have to do some genuinely original thinking. Groping for a lead, Words asks if love of woman is what his "Lord" has in mind. Croak's "Alas !" indicates that this guess is correct and that the subject is going to involve some painful probing into the depths of the artist's character and experience.

Words has some difficulty following this lead, however. Like an analytic philosopher confronted with an aspect of experience that demands for its comprehension a certain amount of imagination and adventurousness, and reluctant to step out into this uncharted area where the guideposts of cliché are no longer present to mark his path, he turns to an examination of language : "(*Very rhetorical.*) Is love the word? . . . Is soul the word? . . . Do we mean love, when we say love? . . . Soul, when we say soul?" (p. 25)

Anguished at this failure of Words, Croak turns once again to Music, who obliges with some *"Love and soul music"* against the protestations of Words. Music is quite willing to plunge head first into areas that lie beyond the realm in which conceptual thought is able to operate comfortably, and in this case he is even able to give fairly adequate, if one-sided, expression to the reality toward which the artist is striving. Still, music alone is not enough for the objectification in full, conscious clarity of a human experience; words are needed too, and the artist has to turn back to them.

In an attempt to give Words some leads that he will more easily be able to follow, Croak suggests "My balms!" and "Age." The experience to be described in tonight's work is that of love contemplated in old age by a man whose loneliness is solaced now only by a few balms, which turn out, as the story unfolds, to be a bed warmed by a warming pan and a sleeping draught of toddy, corrected from arrowroot evidently as more suitable to the rhythm of what is to be the final song.

The process of composition is a laborious one. Words and Music have to experiment with various musical settings even as the verbal sequence is being worked out, and Croak often becomes impatient with them, calling them "Dogs!" and exhorting them to more strenuous endeavour. The love that is described is not given a specific circumstantial setting, nor is it a disembodied abstraction; rather it is the essence of a concrete love that has failed. As the protagonist of the poem sits by the fire waiting for the "hag" (p. 27), evidently an old woman who looks after him, to warm the bed with the pan and to bring him his sleeping draught, he looks into the embers and sees arising from them, out of his memory or imagination, a woman "who loved could not be . . . won or. . . . Or won not loved . . . or some other trouble." Whether, that is, the love she represents was lost through personal failure or through circumstance is not what is important; what is important is that love is no longer a possibility and that now in old age the protagonist perceives its absence as a genuine loss. Like Krapp, the man in the work being created here is a person who feels that he is about to leave life without having benefited from the opportunities life seemed once to have held out to him. He does not have a very precise idea of what this thing is that he has lost, nor does he know whether the loss was his responsibility or whether it happened through circumstance or the nature of things. He does not know because the artist, whose fictional mask he is, does not know. There is only the tentative, groping sense that something has been lost and that this something might have had some connection with a potential relationship with the woman now appearing to his consciousness.

At this point Words trails off into silence. In spite of some brief suggestions from Music, Words can, for the moment, go no further. Instead, the two recapitulate together what has been composed so far, fourteen lines of song :

> Age is when to a man
> Huddled o'er the ingle
> Shivering for the hag
> To put the pan in the bed
> And bring the toddy
> She comes in the ashes
> Who loved could not be won
> Or won not loved
> Or some other trouble
> Comes in the ashes
> Like in that old light
> The face in the ashes
> That old starlight
> On the earth again.

> [p. 28]

This is followed by a long silence, broken finally by Croak's murmur : "The face. . . . The face. . . . The face. . . . The face."

With Music leading the way now into this new area, Words goes on to create the image of a face of "quite . . . piercing beauty," now "a little . . . blunted" (p. 29), the face of a woman with eyes closed, "brows knitted in a groove suggesting pain but simply concentration more likely . . . on some consummate inner process" (p. 30), perhaps coitus, as "the great white rise and fall of the breasts" suggests. As the face takes shape with the details of the description, Croak cries out in anguish : "Lily !" The passion with which this bursts from him makes it clear that the composition this evening is not merely a fiction, but a fictional recreation of some element of the artist's life that is highly charged with emotion for him. Words continues without too much difficulty, evidently impelled by the emotional power associated with this image. He fills in the description of the woman's lips, pressed together, the pallor of her complexion, the rise and fall of her breasts, expressed musically by an *"irrespressible burst of spreading and subsiding music,"* to the climax of this sequence with the opening of her eyes.

The next section describes a penetration through the eyes, like that which Krapp sought in the eyes of the girl in the boat, into the depths of the woman's being. In real life, if this is memory, this penetration was never realized, but now in retrospect the protagonist sees it as something that might have contained the key to what life could have been. The poem describes a descent downward "through the trash" (p. 31), that is, through all the superficial phenomena of the human condition, flesh, sense, will, thought, toward the depths of her noumenal reality, a region "all dark" in which there is

> . . . no begging
> No giving no words
> No sense no need. . . .

down to the heart of her life,

> . . . whence one glimpse
> Of that wellhead.

What does this mean? The meaning is complex and may be only partially true. Like all of Beckett's characters, both those who have fled from reality and those who have sought it where it is not to be found, in concepts, power, and possessions, the old man in the poem, the artist's self-representation in art, has failed to really live, failed to achieve fullness of being, and now as he looks back upon this failure, long after it is too late to correct it, it seems to him that perhaps the way to have penetrated to the "wellhead," the fountain of being, would have been through the heart of another in a personal relationship. Is this a correct guess on his part? The question is difficult, and an answer would depend to a large extent on certain elements of his character that are not disclosed. Perhaps in a genuine emotional interpenetration he might indeed have found what he was seeking; or, and this is equally possible, he might have failed there too, seeking reality in another in order to avoid finding it in himself. He cannot know the answer to these questions, nor can we. The entire inquiry is a tentative guess on his part, and from what we see of him, it looks as if even a positive answer would be merely theoretical; age has closed off all possibility of actual renewal. All that is left is the vision of art, hypothetical and incomplete. The composition having been completed, the vision having been formulated, the artist shuffles away, leaving Words and Music once again alone in the dark.

CHAPTER X

Cascando

Cascando (1963), another radio play, is very close, both in form and in theme, to *Words and Music*.¹ Once again there is an artist in control of words and music, this time called Voice and Music, and once again the artist is seeking to find, through the artistic formulation of a vision in which verbal and musical expression, thought and feeling, would fuse, the answer to the deepest question of his existence : how to be. The difference is that this time the artist is not seeking the answer in a merely theoretical way and in reference to a past that is renounced as unredeemable, nor is there any question of his trying to avoid the problem of his personal existence by finding the answer in another. He does not know whether or not he will reach what he is looking for, but he has hope and is determined to press on toward the goal, whatever the obstacles either within or without. Though his voice is *"dry as dust"* (p. 9), the artist affirms that the time is the month of May, "the reawakening" (p. 15), and not just for nature or for man in general, but for him.

The title, *Cascando,* is an Italian word which means falling, stumbling, falling into ruins, tumbling down. This is the condition both of the "opener" and of the man he describes in his story, Woburn : a condition of ruin and faltering progress. When Woburn falls, as when the artist stumbles in the creation of his story, it does not matter whether he falls "on purpose or not" (p. 11); what matters is that he is down, then up, then goes on.

The voice says that the stories he has told number "thousands and one" (p. 9), that all he ever did with his life was tell stories, hoping each time that the one he was working on would be "the right one," the one that would let him rest. Evidently what he has been looking for is the formulation of a vision that will terminate the restless quest of his mind for reality. Most of Beckett's characters know that concepts and real existence can never fit together, but still they can never stop trying to find a final satisfying concept which will end the intellectual torment that drives them always further. This time, however, the voice has genuine hope that the breakthrough will come, into a mode of vision that will leave concepts behind and arrive at the being of reality itself. "But this one," he says, "it's different . . . I'll finish it . . . then rest . . . it's the right one . . . this time . . . I have it . . . I've got it . . . Woburn." The reason Woburn can be a source of hope is that he is changing, becoming a person who might meet the preconditions for the final vision. He has not yet changed enough, but he is moving in the right direction.

The story describes Woburn's journey. He waits in a shed for night to fall, then steps out into the night to commence his quest. He is wearing the "same old coat" and hat, but he has come to a point of fundamental decision of large symbolic import: ". . . right the sea . . . left the hills . . . he has the choice" (p. 10). The significance of this choice becomes clear as the story proceeds. The land is the place of human habitation, whether of families in homes, strangers at inns, or solitaries in caves. It is the universe that man has domesticated by fitting onto it the harness of his concepts and persuading himself that the harness fits. The sea is untamed, raw reality. Woburn does not make his decision easily. As he stumbles down the slope to the bank, falling occasionally with his face in the mud, then struggling on, he is not certain where he is headed. At one point a "vague memory" comes into his mind of "a hole . . . a shelter . . . a hollow . . . in the dunes . . . a cave" (p. 11), tempting him to withdraw from the quest into one of the old terrestrial shelters that he is now called to outgrow. The temptation does not deter him this time. Finally he makes his way down to the sand and the sea and sets out on the water in a boat.

During all this, the story is interrupted several times by the opener, who speaks of how "they" say that this is only something "in his head" (p. 12). Evidently the artist has been reproached by people who have told him that his concerns, like his stories, are not real, that he does not need the vision he is groping toward and that he is wasting his time trying to create a work that will embody it. Probably they are the kind of people for whom a pot is always and only a pot and who, unlike Watt, can say Pot, pot and be comforted. The artist protests, however, that the concern that shapes this story and that impels him to tell it is not only real but vital to him: "It's my life, I live on that." They continue to denounce him, but he no longer protests; he simply pushes on, like his character: "I don't protest any more, I don't say any more, There is nothing in my head. I don't answer any more. I open and close" (p. 13). And as Woburn proceeds further out into the silence of the sea, leaving behind not only the mainland, but islands as well, the opener becomes progressively more independent of "them": "But I don't answer any more. And they don't say anything any more. They have quit. Good" (p. 16). He is doing his own thinking now, with his own mind, pursuing a goal that he knows he can never reach except alone. The solitude of the quest is not easy to endure, but it is his, and he bears it: "I open. . . . I'm afraid to open. But I must open. So I open" (pp. 16-17). And as he presses closer and closer toward the end, the verbal and musical sequences draw together toward the final vision that will unite them in a fusion of thought and feeling: "From one world to another, it's as though they drew together. We have not much further to go. Good" (p. 15). There was a time when he thought he would not have to give up completely the world of traditional concepts, when he thought the quest could be undertaken as merely an outing from which he could return to the old familiar world, but this time he realizes that all of that must be left behind for good:

> There was a time I asked myself, What is it?
> There were times I answered, It's the outing.
> Two outings.
> Then the return.
> Where?
> To the village.
> To the inn.
> Two outings, then at last the return, to the village, to the inn, by the only road that leads there.
> An image, like any other.
> But I don't answer any more.
> I open.
>
> [pp. 17-18]

Woburn has to leave behind everything that could ever be a comfort to him, and, letting go of all preconceived ideas of his destination, to entrust himself to the sea: "faster . . . scudding . . . rearing . . . plunging . . . heading nowhere . . . heading anywhere . . . lights . . . island astern . . . far astern . . . heading out . . . vast

deep . . . no more land" (pp. 16-17). This is what he has to do, but
although he pursues this to some distance, he finds he still cannot
leave the land entirely behind; he has brought some of it with him,
woven into his own person. He has changed "nearly enough"
(p. 17), but not quite. He still wears the "same old coat" and
"clings on" to the boat as though it were the last outpost of land
left to cling to, and it is probably for this reason that as he lies
"arms spread" in the bottom of the boat, he remains with his "face
in the bilge" so that he cannot see the new realm into which he has
penetrated. Evidently he cannot overcome or let go of his despair
at losing the lights of land, but if he could look up, he would find
that there are other lights as well: "lights gone . . . of the land . . .
all gone . . . nearly all . . . too far . . . too late . . . of the sky
. . . those . . . if you like . . . he need only . . . turn over . . . he'd
see them . . . shine on him . . . but no . . . he clings on . . . Woburn
. . . he's changed . . . nearly enough" (p. 17).

The artist cannot bring this story to its end, but he refuses to
give it up. The play ends with expressions of hope that the end will
come and of determination to press on resolutely toward it: ". . .
we're there . . . nearly . . . just a few more . . . don't let go . . .
Woburn . . . he clings on . . . come on . . . come on" (p. 19)

What would the end be if he could reach it? We are not told,
except that it would have something to do with the acceptance of
starlight as a replacement for the lights of land. In reality, however, even that is "an image, like any other." The vision itself would
lie beyond art, and even the most nearly adequate art could never
contain it. All the artist can do is take us with him on the
approach, but no matter how far the approach proceeds, it will
always be only an approach. Whether either the artist or we
could ever reach the end is a question that is only raised and left
open.

CHAPTER XI

Trios: *Play* and *Come and Go*

Since to follow Woburn further would be beyond the capacity of art, Beckett returns in his subsequent works to a consideration of those who have felt the challenge to Woburn's quest only dimly or not at all, being too preoccupied with the life of the land that Woburn left behind. *Play* (1963) and *Come and Go* (1966)[1] examine characters who, in the one case, have locked themselves in a vicious circle of passions that will not let them respond to the call to clarity that is the challenge at the heart of human existence, and who, in the other, have never proceeded even that far into real living but languish in a kind of living death because, like the little girl Maddy Rooney spoke of in *All That Fall,* they have never been really born. In the process of exploring these themes, these two plays also develop further and make particularly clear an important feature of Beckett's art that has become especially prominent in his later work : his great concern with aesthetic form. All of Beckett's work uses carefully developed formal patterns in its embodiment of his themes, but his most recent work has given the formal element greater emphasis than ever. *How It Is* (1961), for example, deals with essentially the same theme as had *The Unnamable,* but differs from it in its use of an elaborate formal structure closely resembling that of sonata form in music.[2] *Play* and *Come and Go* show a similar emphasis on form, and again there is a parallel to music : both weave three voices in and out of thematic patterns in a manner resembling that of a musical trio.

In *Play,* the three voices are those of a man, his wife, and his mistress, called in the stage directions M, W1, and W2. The play studies the relations among these three characters — a love triangle — and their reactions to the situation they find themselves in after death : forced to think and talk by a light which moves from one to another, opening and closing their streams of voice and weaving them into intricate contrapuntal patterns. As the audience watches and listens to them, the pleasure it derives is both in the perception

113

of aesthetic form and in the perception of the enhanced meaning this form expresses as the three streams reflect upon and illuminate each other.

The work is divided into sections resembling the movements of a piece of music, with themes moving from voice to voice until the voices come together into choruses to open and close the sections. The opening is a chorus on the present situation, a post-mortem state in which the characters find themselves in urns in the dark except for the times when the light shines on them. Although they are side by side, the man in the middle and the two women beside him, they are not conscious of each other, only of themselves, the darkness, and the light. After this opening chorus there is a pause of about five seconds, then another chorus in which all three begin to recount memories of the lives they led on earth. This chorus is stopped almost immediately by another blackout, after which the spot makes them speak individually, shifting back and forth among them. This section presents their memories of the affair, recounted in parallel, and then closes with another blackout (p. 52). One might say that this first movement has a single theme, memory, but transmuted in three different voices according to the opposing points of view of the characters.

The second section, which opens with another chorus, is much more complex. It has two themes, and the voices move from one to the other and back again in a very intricate pattern. The themes are : (1) the present situation and the meaning of the light, and (2) speculations on what might be happening at present on earth. The second is turned to as an escape from the frustration of not being able to solve the problem presented by the first. It is significant that the first to turn to the second theme is the man : he is the weakest willed of the group, the one most inclined now, just as when he was alive, to try to escape from the inhospitable, cold world of reality into the kind of fantasy that he tried to act out in his relationship with his mistress. The second is the mistress, and the last is the toughest, and also most self-centered, of the three, the wife. Schematically presented, the permutations in this movement fall into a pattern like this :

The light (present situation)	The earth (escape)
M, W1, W2	
W1, W2	M
W1	M, W2
M, W2	W1
W1, W2	M
M, W1, W2	

As this diagram makes clear, M is the most inclined of the three to seek escape, and it also might be worth noting that when he is not either by himself or with the group as whole, he tends to associate with W2, his mistress : he always did find her more congenial than his wife.

At the end of this section the opening chorus returns, and the whole play is repeated; then after it closes for the second time it prepares for another repetition, this time with a slight variation — M is going to open instead of W1 — but with no essential change. Evidently as long as the characters cling to the patterns of thought that got them into this situation, they will never break out of it.

However, there are also indications that to break out of it would be possible and that they are actually being challenged to do so. As the light shines on them, setting their streams of consciousness and speech in movement, it seems to them that it is demanding something and that satisfaction of its demand would deliver them finally into silence, darkness, and rest. And that this is not simply idle speculation or self-deluding hope on their parts is indicated by references in the notes to the light as an "inquisitor" and to the characters as its "victims" (p. 62). When the Unnamable, in his own state of life after death, speculated on the possibility of a similar meaning of the lights that were shining on him and forcing him to think and talk, there was nothing to indicate that this hypothesis had any more substance to it than any one of the many others his mind secreted like cobwebs, but in this case the authorial voice has given independent support to the idea.

What, then, is it that the light demands? Since it is an "inquisitor," it must be searching for truth, and the uncovering of this truth would evidently require each character's recognition of the reality of his life. This would involve not only a frank confession of moral deficiencies in the usual sense, of which these characters have plenty, but also the same kind of absolute clarity about existence to which we have seen so many of Beckett's characters called.

As the light probes, their personalities unfold before us. The man, for example, is a vividly earthy character : sexually potent — "What a male!" exclaims his wife at one point (p. 48) on thinking of how he managed to keep both her and the mistress physically satisfied for so long — but weak and vacillating as a person. His polygamous tendency appears to be the result of both of these characteristics : his appetites lead him to take a second woman, and his weakness of character makes it impossible for him to choose between the two no matter how uncomfortable the conflict between them makes him. His ideal would be an affair both women would tolerate, and his fantasies about how pleasant a life of that sort might have been have a languorous quality that corresponds to his intrinsic lassitude. "To think we were never together. . . . Never woke together, on a May morning, the first to wake to wake the other two. Then in a little dinghy . . . on the river, I resting on my oars, they lolling on air-cushions in the stern . . . sheets. Drifting Such fantasies" (pp. 59-60).

His wife, on the other hand, is a very active, fiercely aggressive person. She lives for personal power, and her husband's value to her seems to be largely that of a possession, an object over which she can assert absolute power. Characteristically, her highest idea of happiness during the part of her life she recounts was to be able to lay claim to uncontested ownership over him : "So he was mine again. All mine. I was happy again. I went about singing. The world — " (p. 51). The world was in her possession, she probably means. And in her exuberance at the victory of her power, she even, characteristically again, went to the mistress to gloat over her in her defeat. In fact, victory seems to have been even sweeter to her than peaceful possession without battle would have been, since it gave her a new instrument to use against her husband to reduce him to complete submission. M remembers how she used to torment him with it and how he used to knuckle under : "I ran into your ex-doxy, she said one night, on the pillow, you're well out of that. Rather uncalled for, I thought. I am indeed, sweetheart, I said, I am indeed. God what vermin women. Thanks to you, angel, I said" (p. 51).

The mistress is the most sensitive of the group and the most concerned with specifically personal relationships, as compared with the relatively impersonal kind of relationship one has with possessions or slaves. It was this that made her become entangled with M, and it was for the sake of a more adequate personal relationship, rather than for the sake of a greater degree of power, that she wanted M to choose her exclusively in place of his wife. And now, in the state after death, the same tendency makes her seek a relationship with the light; always having been a person who lived for the eyes of others, she tries to imagine the light as looking upon her with personal concern, feeling anger, sympathy, and so on :

> You might get angry and blaze me clean out of my wits. Mightn't you? . . . But I doubt it. It would not be like you somehow. And you must know I am doing my best. Or don't you? . . . Are you listening to me? Is anyone listening to me? Is anyone looking at me? Is anyone bothering about me at all?
>
> [PP. 54-55]

Perhaps it is because of her greater sensitivity and the consequently greater sense of loneliness that this speech reflects that she is the only one of the three to go mad at the end of the cycle.

The wife, shrewish as ever, is less inclined to wheedle with the light and more inclined to assert herself against it. Like the others, she speculates about the idea that perhaps it is demanding a confession from her, but she is less inclined to ask it what it wants and more inclined to rely on her own powers of reasoning for the answer : "I can do nothing . . . for anybody . . . any more . . . thank God. So it must be something I have to say. How the mind works still !" (p. 54). And of the three, she is the only one who dares to order the light to leave her alone : 'Get off me !" (p. 53).

The man thinks about what the light might want — "Am I hiding something? Have I lost . . . the thing you want?" (pp. 57-58). But, like the vacillating person he is, he spends most of his time indulging in memories or fantasies and avoiding the problem of what it is he might be hiding which when brought forth might lead to a more permanent and satisfying peace than that of his customary escapes.

From what we see, it does not look as if any of them will ever find real peace. The repetition of the play indicates that they are are all far too deeply entrenched in these patterns of thought ever to find their way out of them. If this is a hell, as the wife's reference to "hellish half-light" (p. 53) suggests, then hell is the necessity of being stuck forever with the superficial identity one has forged for oneself by one's life.

Come and Go is a still more sparely formal work; in fact it is almost as close as the theater can get to pure form, since it is about almost — though not quite — nothing. The notes at the end describing the patterns of the successive positions of the three characters as they come and go, the pattern of their crossed hands, the lighting, costumes, and so on, contain about half again as many words as the text, which is itself little more than a highly symmetrical arrangement of repetitions, such as: "Does she not realize?", "God grant not"; "Has she not been told?", "God forbid"; "Does she not know?", "Please God not."

The subject — what little there is — is the pallidness of life in those who never manage, for one reason or another, to engage in more than a shadowy existence on the fringe of active life. Since they are all in the same situation, all, that is, in the same state of half-life, Flo, Vi, and Ru all look pretty much alike. Although they wear different colors, their clothes are in every other way identical. They are of "undeterminable" age, like the living ghosts they are, and they speak in "colourless" voices "as low as compatible with audibility" and move on and off in complete silence.

Whether they are still alive in middle or old age, or whether, like the characters in *Play*, they are in an after-death state looking back on the world, is not specified. Nor is it of any importance. All that matters is that life has slipped past them and that now they meet occasionally to comfort each other over its loss. Evidently they were once girls together at school — they remember sitting on a log "in the playground at Miss Wade's" — and evidently they have never had any subsequent life worth mentioning, since they never mention one. The action consists simply in each going off to one side for a moment while the ones who remain whisper in each other's ears some secret they are keeping from the one who is absent. We are never told what the secret is — that they are dead? that there is no more hope of marriage? or simply that the absent one has her lipstick on wrong or that she has a pimple on her nose? — but again it is not particularly important; the essential situation remains the same whatever the secret. The secret itself is simply an instrument by which two attempt to fabricate an illusion of common concern and of power over the one who is excluded.

After they finish their routine of exits and whisperings, involving the changes of seating diagrammed in the end notes, they sit and clasp hands in a crisscross pattern, and one says, "I can feel the rings." Since the notes say their hands are clearly visible and that there are no rings apparent, it appears that like so many others in the world of Beckett's plays, they are comforting themselves with an illusion, perhaps the illusion that they are wearing engagement rings — promising the opportunity of a life to come — or that they are widowed and have their wedding rings left as a testimony to the fullness of life that was once theirs. Whichever it is, and it could be vague enough in their minds to be both, it is only a dream, just as in the old days at Miss Wade's when they used to sit holding hands, "dreaming of . . . love." There are no rings, they have not lived, and they never will.

CHAPTER XII

Film

Film (1965) is Beckett's only work created specifically for the
cinematic medium, and it is also the only work for which he has
written — in the notes and in the general directions for production
— an extensive critical exposition.[1] Even here, as one might expect,
he stops short of unequivocally endorsing his own commentary:
"No truth value attaches to above," he says, "regarded as of merely
structural and dramatic convenience" (p. 75). What he means, however, is not that his comments are false, but only that they describe
what some might call a phenomenological reality, not ultimate
reality but rather the appearance that constitutes man's experience
of reality. If we keep this reservation in mind, we can understand
properly the intent of his comments. He tells us that the film is
about perception and self-perception, that, in Berkeley's phrase,
"esse est percipi" (to be is to be perceived),[2] and that to seek nonbeing by fleeing from the eyes of others is futile, since self-
perception is inescapable. It is easy to see why Beckett would take
care to disclaim any effort to express metaphysical truth of the type
in which Berkeley was interested; he is himself far closer to Hume
than to Berkeley, and he probably well remembers what Hume did
to Berkeley's metaphysics. What Beckett is concerned to give us is
not ontology, but simply a description of what flight from a too
acute awareness of reality feels and looks like.

To represent this flight from perception dramatically, the film
divides its protagonist into two elements: object (O) and eye (E). O
is in flight from E, and E is in pursuit of O. It is established as a
convention of the work that when E's angle of view of O, whom he
normally sees from behind, is greater than 45°, O becomes uncomfortably aware of being perceived and either flees or turns away to
reduce the angle. There are a number of differences between the
text and the final film, but in my discussion I will be concerned
mainly with the text, since it represents more closely Beckett's
original conception of the work. The text — though not the film

as produced[3] — begins with a street scene in which various people, all going in the same direction and all in pairs, are proceeding unhurriedly about their business. All are "contentedly in *percipere* and *percipi*" (p. 77), which indicates that it is only a person who, like O-E, is perilously close to really clear perception who will find either *percipere* or *percipi* disturbing. These people are peacefully engrossed in the roles they play in life and consequently remain comfortably remote from real selfhood. When O appears, he is hurrying along in the opposite direction. In contrast to the others, whose acceptance of the surface of life is represented by the light summer clothing that exposes them to the day, O is bundled up in a long dark overcoat with his hat pulled down over his eyes. On his left he hugs the wall, and on his right he shields the exposed side of his face with his hand.

As O rushes along in "blind haste" (p. 77), he jostles "an elderly couple of shabby genteel aspect" who are standing on the sidewalk looking at a newspaper together, an activity that represents their complacent participation in the kind of superficial, collective life in which people join together in thinking the thoughts that everybody thinks everybody else is thinking. It is probably significant in this respect that in the actual film the man is wearing a clerical collar; this identifies him as one of the official custodians of conventional beliefs and values. Though O hurries on past, E stops for a moment to look at the couple. At first they are not aware of E's presence, but slowly they become uncomfortable as they feel his gaze upon them. When they finally turn and look directly at him, there gradually comes over their faces "an expression only to be described as corresponding to an agony of perceivedness" (p. 78). Evidently people can remain quite comfortable in their conventional lives as long as they are never exposed to a really clear perception of themselves, but become acutely anxious when genuine clarity illumines them. Even when it comes from the eye of another fugitive, it makes them uncomfortably conscious of something in themselves from which they have been fleeing. Their pet monkey, in contrast, is completely indifferent; only man has the gift, and the burden, of being able to hide from reality in self-deception. Overcome with anxiety, the man and woman close their eyes and hurry away in the same direction as all the others, the opposite of that in which O and E are moving. A few moments later the same expression of horror comes over the face of a flower-woman E looks at as he is pursuing O up the stairs of a building. She closes her eyes and collapses among her flowers, as E turns again and hurries on to overtake O, who is on his way to a room.

E is directly behind O when O unlocks the door of the room and enters. Here the point of view shifts to O. The way this is signalled in the film is that when the point of view is O's, the image is slightly fuzzy in contrast to the sharp vision of E. During the subsequent episode the point of view moves back and forth between O and E several times. Upon entering, O locks the door behind him, then turns and surveys the room. What he sees are : a dog and cat, a mirror, a window, a couch with rug, a parrot, a goldfish, and a rocking chair. First he sets down the briefcase he has been carrying, then goes to the window and draws the curtain. Next he takes up the rug and covers the mirror with it. Bothered by the eyes of the dog and cat, which have been staring at him during this sequence, he takes them and puts them out of the room. After all these matters are taken care of he evidently feels that he will be able to devote himself without further disturbance to the business immediately on his mind. However, when he takes his briefcase and sits down in the rocker to open it, he finds himself distracted by the eyes of God the Father "staring at him severely" from a print on the wall. After getting up and tearing this to pieces and grinding the pieces underfoot, he returns to his seat and removes from the briefcase a folder, which he is about to open when he is disturbed once again, this time by the eye of the parrot. He gets up and covers the parrot's cage with his coat, then becomes aware of the eye of the fish and covers the bowl as well.[4] Finally he settles down, removing his hat so that a narrow band of elastic encircling the head is revealed to E, and takes from the folder a packet of photographs.

The photographs show a series of seven scenes from O-E's past. All are pictures of him in various circumstances and at various important stages of his life. The first shows him at six months in his mother's arms. His mother in a "big old-fashioned beflowered hat" is looking down at him, "her severe eyes devouring him" (p. 88). Evidently he has always felt some fear of being devoured by those eyes, and it is perhaps in part the power of this fascination with his mother and her mode of vision that has brought him here to relive his life in the inspection of these photographs. Although it is not certain, it would seem likely that the room is his mother's.[5] It seems fairly clear that it is not his — he would hardly be likely to fill a room of his own with so many disturbing eyes — and since his mother, as the next picture makes clear, was a religious believer, she would seem a more likely person to have put up the picture of God the Father. If this is the case, perhaps O feels that by returning to his mother's world, the source of his existence, he may be able to reach a better understanding of the shape of his own life and in the process find a means of escape from it.

The second photograph gives an idea of the kind of influence his mother had on him. He is four years old, dressed in a night shirt, on a veranda, kneeling on a cushion in an attitude of prayer at the knees of his mother, who, wearing another hat similar to the one in the first photograph, bends over him with "severe eyes."[6] Evidently she is teaching him to pray in the old-fashioned way to the old-fashioned God who corresponds to the old-fashioned style of her hat.[7]

It was in this manner that her "devouring" eyes tried to absorb him into their way of viewing the universe, and the rebellion against their vision has evidently been one of the principal motivating forces of his subsequent life. To see with one's own eyes, however, is an almost impossible, and perhaps unendurable, task, and if he has been running away from his mother's eyes, he has also been fleeing his own. It is his own, in E, that are now about to take possession of him, and it is evidently in part his rebellion against the eyes of his mother that has now made him the prey of E. In Beckett's world to attempt to do one's own thinking is dangerous: the attempt sometimes puts one in the position of having actually to do it.

From the following photographs it appears that the world into which his mother's womb ejected him at his birth has proved even more difficult to escape than her eyes. The third shows some of the temptations life uses to entrap one. Here the protagonist is 15 years old and smiling. He is evidently enjoying the dignity that his school blazer and his progress toward manhood give him, and he is engaging in one of the more delicious of life's temptations: power. He is teaching a dog to sit up on its hind legs and beg. In the fourth he is twenty and smiling still as he stands on a platform in an academic gown to receive his diploma. In the background is a "section of public watching." From all indications he seems about to launch out on his own in a comfortably public personality, living the life and thinking the thoughts of the kind of people we saw earlier on the street.

Whereas the first four photographs each took O about six seconds to examine, the next two he stops over for twelve. Apparently they arouse particularly strong emotions because of their association with the deepest entanglements into which life managed to lead him before he turned around for good to run in the opposite direction from that of the world. In the fifth he is twenty-one and still smiling, with his arm around his fiancée. A small moustache indicates both his acceptance of and his pride in the role to which manhood has called him. In the next he is twenty-five, with a larger moustache and still smiling, holding in his arms a little girl, evidently his daughter. O must still feel some attachment to the child, since he reaches out and touches her face with his forefinger. The fact that he is in military uniform, "newly enlisted," suggests that at the time of the photograph he was about to go off to war. The uniform in the photograph used in the actual film looks like the type worn in World War I.

The final photograph holds O only six seconds again, probably because it represents something with which he is already quite familiar: the man he has become. He is thirty in this picture, but looks over forty. He has on an overcoat and, in contrast to his bareheadedness in all the previous pictures, a hat, which would seem to represent both the achievement of his mature identity and a defense against exposure to life.[8] He is cleanshaven now, suggesting that he has rejected the role of lover and father with which the moustache was associated, and he has a patch over his left eye, perhaps indicating that he was mutilated in the war. His face has a grim expression.

When O has finished looking at the seventh photograph, he tears it into four pieces and drops them on the floor, then goes back through each of the earlier ones and does the same, ending with the first, which is on a heavier mount and requires greater effort but which finally gives beneath his straining hands. In destroying all of these images of himself, he evidently believes that he is annihilating not only his memories, but also the selfhood that is such a burden to him. When he has finished this, he leans back in the rocker, holding onto the armrests, and tries to go to sleep. The self he has tried to destroy, however, is only a phenomenal one, and in freeing himself from it, or giving himself the illusion of freedom from it, he has only laid himself open to a far more dangerous adversary : the noumenal reality, E, which lies behind it. The attempt to flee from self-perception has ironically led him to tear down the principal defense which shielded him from it.

In the final scene, E slowly moves around for a full view of O, though furtively and with occasional retreats as O reacts to the sense of his presence. When O finally falls into a deep sleep, E is able to work his way around to a position directly in front of him for a long look at his sleeping face, which is seen to have a patch over the left eye. Then suddenly E's gaze wakes O, who starts and stares up at him. O clutches the armrests and stiffens, and gradually the expression of the "agony of perceivedness" comes over him. The next image is E as seen by O : "It is O's face (with patch) but with a very different expression, impossible to describe, neither severity nor benignity, but rather acute *intentness*. A big nail is visible near left temple (patch side). Long image of the unblinking gaze" (p. 83). Finally O, horrified, closes his eyes and covers his face with his hands.

What does this image of E signify? The calm, intent gaze would appear to correspond to the gentle, but unyielding persistence with which E has pursued his perception of O, and the absence of emotion in his face suggests a fundamental detachment on the part of this deepest level of O-E's reality from the violent reactions of his superficial, phenomenal identity. The large nail in his left temple, however, suggests that, as E is a part of O, he has not been completely immune to the effects that O's approach to life has had on his total self. The nail in the temple evidently signifies a wound that has penetrated to the core of O-E's being. Exactly what kind, however, is not specified in the text. Perhaps as an image the nail has some connection with the tent-peg Jael, Heber's wife, is said to have driven through the temple of Sisera, a Canaanite captain, in a story recounted in the book of Judges. Sisera, having lost a battle with the Israelites, fled from his pursuers and asked Jael to hide him in her tent. She promised to do so, but later, while he was sleeping, she "took a nail of the tent, and took an hammer in her hand, and went softly unto him, and smote the nail into his temples" (Judg. 4 :21). Sisera died, of course, and perhaps the parallel is intended to indicate that O-E in his flight from life has received a mortal wound that will eventually destroy him completely. At any rate, the nail in E's temple suggests that even if the clear gaze of the inner reality of the self could under some circumstances have healing power, it probably will not under these; the damage that has been done has already penetrated too deep. Perhaps if O and E could be united in a single vision, the larger self of which the two are both indispensable parts could be healed of the inner division that is destroying it, but if this is true, it can in this case be true only in a theoretical way, since O is not capable of opening himself to this vision. The film ends with the two still separated, E watching and O locked away from him in his horror.

CHAPTER XIII

Eh Joe

Joe, the protagonist of *Eh Joe* (1966), Beckett's first television play, is another man in flight.[1] Like Henry, in *Embers*, he hears speaking inside him voices from the past, in this case the voice of one of the many women to whom he has made love, and like O, in *Film*, he has been trying to escape from himself by destroying the memories that keep his past alive in him. And again like O, he makes the ironic mistake of working his way into the very trap he is trying to avoid. In violently silencing one by one the voices that have hounded him, tormenting him with memories, he has been stripping away without realizing it the veils that have shielded him from the direct vision he has been trying to escape. The play presents him at the point at which this terrifying truth is just beginning to dawn on him. He is still running, and he has not yet been finally caught, but he is beginning to realize that when the last voice goes silent for good, he will be. Consequently, whereas he has deliberately stifled all of the previous voices, he now begins to fear the dying out of the present one, and as it grows gradually weaker during the play, instead of willing it to end, he strains to hear the words that still come through. Like E in *Film*, the camera in this play seems to represent the protagonist's self-perception; it approaches closer when the voice goes silent, but stops when the voice resumes.

When the play begins, Joe, in his late fifties and gray-haired, is sitting alone in his room on the edge of his bed in an old dressing gown and slippers. He has a hunted look as he sits in an *"intent pose"* (p. 35), then gets up, checks the window to make sure no one is outside, draws the curtain, goes on to the door and checks it in the same way, locks it, goes to the cupboard and does the same, and even kneels to look under the bed before sitting down once again. Evidently these precautions give him some feeling of security, because after completing them he is finally able to begin to relax. This does not last long, however; when the woman's voice opens, the tension immediately comes back into his features. During the remainder of the play this visible tension subsides and resumes in parallel with the pauses and resumptions of the voice.

The voice, which seems to have a clearer understanding of Joe than he himself — or perhaps one should say his *conscious* self — does, knows the real futility of these maneuvers of his and mocks them : "Thought of everything? . . . Forgotten nothing? . . . You're all right now, eh? . . . No one can see you now. . . . Why don't you put out that light? . . . There might be a louse watching you" (p. 36). After the camera moves in a little closer, she reminds him of who she is and what her relationship with him was : "The best's to come, you said, that last time . . . Hurrying me into my coat" (pp. 36-37). Evidently that line was one Joe used with many of the women he loved and left, since the voice reminds him somewhat later of how he said the same thing to another girl who committed suicide afterwards : "The best's to come, you said. . . . Ticket in your pocket for the first morning flight" (p. 39). The phrase which Joe used deceptively as a means of manipulating his women has now come home to roost, as the voice points out, with a new meaning he did not foresee : having destroyed all the relationships which might have preserved him from the isolation that would finally leave him prey to himself, he is now condemned to await precisely that. The voice taunts him with the irony of the fate he has made for himself : "Say it now, Joe. . . . say it again now and listen to yourself . . . The best's to come . . . You were right for once . . . In the end" (p.37).

Then after another advance by the camera, she takes up the subject of her mode of being in his mind, making clear that even if her reality is a mental one, she is nevertheless genuinely real. Evidently Joe has always managed to escape his voices by persuading himself they were *merely* mental and consequently could be dismissed :

You know that penny farthing hell you call your mind . . . That's where you think this is coming from, don't you? . . . That's where you heard your father. . . . Started in on you one June night and went on for years . . . On and off . . . Behind the eyes . . . That's how you were able to throttle him in the end . . . Mental thugee you called it. . . . Otherwise he'd be plaguing you yet.

[p. 37]

From the persistence of the voices, one springing up to replace another, it appears that if they are within him they are also independent of him in the sense that they are beyond his power to
control consciously, and if this woman's voice is typical, it would
seem that they have more power over him than he over them.
Evidently the voices are masks that a deeper level of his mind uses
to try to call his attention to certain truths about himself that are
tied up with the memories they represent. This woman, for example,
has as her special message the self-centered isolation to which his
way of life has brought him, and this is a truth he is going to have
to face whether he wishes to or not. "Throttling the dead in his
head" (p. 37) cannot destroy the reality to which the living
memories of the dead are pointing him. In fact, she says, when he
eventually finds that he has driven away not only all the people
who ever cared about him but also their voices in his mind, he is
going to discover that to be alone is the worst horror of all:
"Watch yourself you don't run short, Joe . . . Ever think of that?
. . . Eh Joe? . . . What'd it be if you ran out of us . . . Not another
soul to still . . . Sit there in his stinking old wrapper hearing himself . . . That lifelong adorer . . . Weaker and weaker till not a gasp
left there either" (p. 37).

Her own voice, she reminds him, was once as strong in his mind
as it was in real life, but now it is "squeezed down to this" (p. 38),
a voice that, according to the stage directions, is low, remote, and
colorless, and she predicts that as it fades further and further into
a whisper, he will cling desperately to what remains of it: "How
much longer would you say? . . . Till the whisper. . . . When you
can't hear the words . . . just the odd one here and there. . . . The
odd word . . . Straining to hear." This prediction comes true, of
course, before the play ends; her voice gradually fades away so that
only the odd italicized word here and there comes through clearly.
It is ironic, she suggests, that when Joe is "nearly home" — that
is, alone with the sole object of his worship, himself — he should
cling to her, whom in real life he rejected in favor of his "Lord."
And she seems to enjoy rubbing in the fact that while she, after he
had rejected her, found somebody else "preferable in all respects"
(p. 39), Joe himself is going to have to endure the punishment of
getting precisely what he asked for: "How's your Lord these days?
. . . Still worth having? . . . Still lapping it up? . . . The passion of
our Joe . . . Wait till He starts talking to you . . . When you're

E

done with yourself . . . All your dead dead. . . . Put your thugs on that . . . Eh Joe? . . . Ever think of that?" (p. 39). What she means is evidently that when Joe manages to disentangle himself once and for all from the memories that have made up what he has thought of as his life, the kind of selfhood that O in *Film* associated with his photographs, he is going to find that the real core of his self is as disturbing to confront as E was to O.

As the woman's voice gradually fades, the play ends with a description in poignant detail of the suicide of the other girl. "There was love for you," she says, tantalizing him with the long ago rejected and now irrevocably lost opportunity for a relationship which, by the strength of the girl's passion for him, might have endured, and which if it had, might have shielded him from the end which is now irresistibly approaching.

CHAPTER XIV

A General View

Now that we have examined each of Beckett's plays in an order roughly corresponding to their chronology, where do we find this has brought us? At the end of a study of Beckett's novels it would probably not seem necessary to ask such a question; in the novels there is a clear line of development which gradually unfolds the implications of certain key ideas. As the reader moves from the earlier fiction to the later, he sees each work as a logical step in a process of thought, and when he arrives at the end, in *The Unnamable* and *How It Is,* he knows where he is and how he came there. The plays, however, fall into a very different pattern. Instead of developing in a continuous line according to the internal logic of a set of ideas, they walk around and around a central problem, trying to describe all sides of it. This problem is the meaning of human life : what it is, how it has become what it is, and what it might become.

These are not entirely different questions from those the novels study, but there is an important difference of emphasis. The novels tend to focus on man's need to know and on the inevitable frustration of this need due to the failure of the philosophical systems he relies on for its satisfaction. The various protagonists of the fiction are all men who at one time or another have studied traditions of systematic thought and who either labor still under the illusion that they can fit their ideas onto reality or else have only recently passed through a slow and painful process of disillusionment with knowledge. Molloy's description of his intellectual background presents a fairly typical picture :

Yes, I once took an interest in astronomy, I don't deny it. Then it was geology that killed a few years for me. The next pain in the balls was anthropology and the other disciplines, such as psychiatry, that are connected with it, disconnected, then connected again, according to the latest discoveries.[1]

131

Some, like Molloy, appear to have been professional scholars at one time, while others, such as Moran, are amateurs, but almost all have put into their philosophical and theological speculations the intensity of passion of those for whom understanding is no mere luxury but a matter of life or death. What the novels are mainly concerned to show is the breakdown of the patterns on which these men pin their hopes and the agonizing frustration into which this throws them. These characters recapitulate in their own lives the history of human thought recounted in the introduction to this book, the history of man's futile attempts to reduce being to idea.

The plays also give attention to man's need to know, and in some plays — *Waiting for Godot,* for example — it is almost the whole idea, but as a group they do not take this as their main concern. This is probably why Beckett said in Berlin in 1967 as he was preparing to direct a production of *Endgame* that the way to understand his plays is to talk "not about philosophy, but about situations."[2] The plays are explorations into the meaning of human life as it is in its full reality, and this meaning is not an abstract idea of the kind that can be known objectively with the intellect, but a mystery that is lived in with the whole self. Consequently although they are concerned in part with philosophical problems, they are concerned even more with the psychology — using this word in a very broad sense — of concrete individuals. They take up situations and probe into them to uncover the human reality that lies in their depths. As they do this, the plays tend to emphasize one or the other of two approaches : analysis or exploration. That is, they tend either to concentrate on the present situation and the causes that have produced it or to examine not only that but also the process of development that is taking place within the present situation and leading beyond it. The extent to which one approach is emphasized over the other is a matter of degree. Some plays focus almost entirely on the present and past and see no future at all that could be in any significant way different; some see changes taking place, but with little or no hope that they will ever come to fruition; and others look mainly toward a future which, though unknown and disturbing, shows signs of promise.

The plays that emphasize analysis study a situation that is fixed, or at least relatively stable. There is virtually no hope of change, either because the situation is inevitable by nature or because the patterns of habit that have caused it and that give it its shape have become too solid to admit disruption. And sometimes it looks as if both causes are present simultaneously. *Act Without Words II* and *Come and Go*, for example, both portray very simple and definite situations that appear to be simultaneously inevitable and habitual. In the first, the goad seems to be a part of the very nature of things, while the habits of living of those who are affected by the goad vary according to the individual. In the second the spinsterhood of the three women appears to be the result both of a lack of opportunity and of a habitual timidity of spirit that would have prevented them from taking advantage of an opportunity if one had come along. In both of these cases, however, since the plays are very brief, the emphasis has to fall on what is fixed. There simply is not room to consider the possibility of alternatives.

Play is longer and more complicated, but once again the emphasis is on what is fixed in the situation. We see only what the characters are, not how they have become what they are, and consequently we have no information about whether other possibilities were ever really open to them. We know only that they are locked forever in patterns of thought and will that are the direct continuation of those that governed their earthly lives. In *Eh Joe*, similarly, the protagonist seems never to have been very different from the person he is when we see him, and there is no special reason to suppose he ever will be. When his voices fade out for good, leaving him alone with himself, it looks as if the change in his situation will be approximately that of the three characters in *Play* after their deaths — which is to say, no essential change at all. He has always been isolated in a narrow self-interest and will probably continue to be.

Krapp's Last Tape and *Embers* show how a person becomes a Joe by choices made over a long period of time. How free the choices of the characters were, however, is another matter : these may have been determined by irresistible inherent weaknesses in their nature. And how much good a different approach to life would have been to them is also uncertain. A person's situation is a combination of what he is and what his world is. If a person chooses to cut himself off from life by egocentricity, intellectual fastidiousness, timidity, or laziness, the world will do him no good at all, however pleasant a place it might be in itself. But if the world has nothing to offer, openness to it will not do much good either. Perhaps Krapp might have found some distraction from loneliness if he had chosen to settle down with one of his women, but if she had turned out to be like Henry's Ada, he would probably have ended up wishing he had stayed in his old room with his tapes. If life has no depths, then a person who wants to live it deeply will be doomed to frustration no matter what choice he makes.

All That Fall presents a larger and more varied world than those that Krapp and Henry live in, but still the situation is not especially different. There are more people, so that we see a greater range of individual choices, but in most cases the object of choice is essentially the same. Most men and women in Boghill, though they walk their own paths, are all pursuing one goal : to live on the surface of life, comfortable in their illusions of dignity, power, and possession. A few become dissatisfied with this superficial life and see through the illusions that sustain it, but only to discover, to their despair, the emptiness that lies beneath. Dan and Maddy Rooney, for all of the differences in their basic attitudes toward life, both arrive at the same disillusionment, and both are destroyed by it. A person who would like a life of greater depth than that of Boghill cannot know where to find it. Freedom would be freedom only to turn from what exists to a hope not merely without possibility, but without even any clear shape.

The situation of the characters of *Waiting for Godot* is similar. They are faced with a choice between illusory meaning and a vision of meaninglessness. Since they do not seem able to endure the latter for more than a few moments, however, they seem even less free than Dan and Maddy. Pozzo's compulsion to keep going on and Vladimir's retreat into the illusion of waiting for Godot both seem to grow out of an irresistible tendency inherent in human nature : the need for meaning. Still, would the freedom to choose to face the vision of meaninglessness be of any value to them? There is nothing in the play to indicate that it would, and if *All That Fall* can be taken as a further unfolding of the implications of *Godot,* it appears that it certainly would not. Clarity can be of no great value if it leads only to despair.

In none of the plays examined above is there any indication that a life different from that which the characters have chosen or been forced into by nature or circumstance could ever have been a practical possibility. Two other plays, though they do not attempt to describe alternative ways of life in any detail, do leave open the possibility that some alternatives might not necessarily lead to a dead end. In *Words and Music,* Croak considers the possibility that a life with the woman in his song, or someone like her, might have been preferable to the lonely life he has lived, and since there is nothing in the play that either explicitly or implicitly denies this possibility, as there was in *Krapp's Last Tape* and *Embers,* hope is not excluded. The possibility is simply examined, not judged. In *Act Without Words I,* the man in the desert seems finally to learn from all his frustrations a stoical resignation which may perhaps deliver him from some of the pain of unsatisfied desire. We cannot see inside him, since there is no dialogue in which the intricacies of his inner life could be revealed, but he does seem at the end to have developed an inner strength that gives him a certain serenity. The two plays point in different directions for solutions to the problems of how to live, but both remain open to the possibility of at least a partial solution.

The plays of exploration probe deeper into this problem and examine it in greater detail. Like the plays of analysis, they are concerned with situations that have taken on a certain shape due to choice or circumstance, and they are interested in determining both the shape and its causes, but the situations they study also contain elements of instability due to obscure processes of change that are taking place within certain characters. These changes are not subject to the control of the characters in which they emerge; they seem to be completely unexpected and, in fact, to be completely contrary to the characters' desires. A character seems free to resist the change or to cooperate with it, but that is about all the freedom he has.

What these processes of change lead toward is a difficult question, especially since we are never shown one that has reached its goal. As the contrast between *Act Without Words I* and *Words and Music* suggested, there seem to be two possible alternatives : isolation and communion. These would appear to be mutually exclusive, but since we see the process of change only in its relatively early stages we have no way of knowing how the two poles would relate in the end. Perhaps they would converge. In every case, the change involves the development of a new, more authentic and individual way of seeing reality, and it stands to reason that withdrawal from the world of collective thought would be a necessary preliminary to this. To see reality as it is, a person would have to see it with his own eyes and without the mediation of preconceived ideas that have been devised by the mass mind more to obscure reality than to illumine it. Since this withdrawal would be, however, from a false community dedicated to a life of illusion, it would really involve the rejection not of communion as such, but only of a superficial imitation of it. Consequently the same isolation that is required for growth into the vision of reality would also seem to be required for the development of authentic communion : men will be one in truth, or they will be one in a lie.

This, at any rate, is a possible projection of the line of development, of which we see the beginnings in the plays of exploration. The ultimate goal of the process they describe, however, lies in the distance, far beyond the territory they cover, and its complete revelation, if there is ever to be one, could come only in plays that Beckett has not yet written. In the meantime we can only speculate in a small way, and cautiously, and attend to what he has given us : a picture of the early stages of the process.

In *Happy Days* and *Film* the change taking place in the central characters involves the emergence from within of new eyes that would see life in a new way, but in both cases the change is resisted and the process is consequently aborted. Winnie senses what is happening, but is disturbed by it and prefers to postpone its fulfillment : "Eyes float up that seem to close in peace . . . to see . . . in peace. . . . Not mine. . . . Not now. . . . No no" (*Happy Days*, p. 51). In *Film*, O is pursued by an inner eye, E, which is much more insistent than that which Winnie felt emerging, but which he resists with a correspondingly greater strength and horror.

In *Cascando* and *Endgame,* on the other hand, though the characters in whom the change is taking place are just as disturbed by it as Winne and O, they are more inclined to cooperate with it. Clov cooperates, or seems to, rather hesitantly, and Woburn's narrator rather more determinedly, but both are at least partially willing to let themelves be led by it to whatever it will take them to, whether to death or to new life. Neither play, however, follows them very far, perhaps because the author himself is still not certain of the exact nature of the ultimate goal toward which their paths lead. Asked in Berlin in 1967 in connection with his production of *Endgame* whether he was of the opinion that an author must have a solution for the riddle of his play, Beckett answered, "Not for this play's."[3]

There may be several reasons why Beckett would say he does not
have an answer to the riddle of *Endgame*. It is clear that something new is happening in this play as in the other plays of exploration, but perhaps to know in any very substantial way what it is
one would have to travel its road oneself. And perhaps even then to
say in explicit terms what end that road leads to would be impossible because this would be a vision and a life that lie beyond
"effing and conating" altogether. This at least is what the hints we
are given seem to suggest. It would not be an answer that could be
formulated because it would be not so much something you look
at as something you are. If this is the case, it would mean that the
answer would require an inner transformation of the person who
would find it, a transformation that would have both moral, or
psychological, and philosophical aspects.

This, of course, brings us to a question that is perhaps indiscreet
to raise and that would be even more indiscreet to try to answer in
any great detail : the relationship between Beckett's art and his life.
At the same time, it is a question that we cannot simply ignore. If
his plays are explorations into reality and not merely hypothetical
abstractions — and there are few plays in the entire history of
literature that have a greater feeling of urgency and seriousness —
then they must be concerned with the reality of concrete life. On
the other hand, however, it would probably be not only risky but
misleading as well to try to identify characters and events in
Beckett's writings with people and incidents in his own life. There
may be some relationships of this sort — Mother Pegg in *Endgame*
as a parellel to Peggy Guggenheim in Beckett's life is an enticing
association, as is the similarity between photograph number two as
described in the text of *Film* and a real photograph of Beckett as
a child kneeling at his mother's knee[4] — but there is nothing they
could tell us that would not be for the most part beside the point.
The relationship between Beckett's works and his own life is probably more like that between his characters and the stories they tell.
The stories of Hamm, Winnie, Croak, Henry, the Opener in *Cascando*, and even Krapp, whose *Effie* is not described to us but
which would seem to have some relationship to the real Effie he
knew, all seem to be based to a certain extent on real incidents in
the lives of their authors or at least to involve some projection of
the author into his protagonist, but the real function of these tales
is not to list the historical incidents of the author's life : it is to

disclose its character. That Winnie was really attacked in her child-
hood by a mouse like that which attacks her Millie would in itself
be meaningless even if it could be proven true; what it shows that
is important, however, is her fear of the destruction she feels would
follow upon her being seen stripped of protective coverings. The
reality in Winnie's life that this story reflects is the threat of being
seen by the eyes from within. Similarly, the historicity of Hamm's
Christmas Eve story is less important than the present truth it
points to : his hatred of life.

In the same way, we must conclude that the significant element
in the relationship between Beckett's work and his life is not to be
found in parallelism of incidents, but in the meaning which the
stories embody. In studying the characters he creates, Beckett is
studying the heart of man — which is his own heart as well. This
means he is not writing in a detached and hypothetical way, aloof
from his artifact, but that he is himself intimately involved both
in the quest his characters pursue and in the weaknesses that prevent them from pursuing it to its end.

So perhaps one reason Beckett would not have an answer to his
own riddle is that he has not yet himself arrived at the point at
which the seeker could become transformed into that answer.

But can we gather nothing of what this transformation would
involve? What about its philosophical aspect? Here too we are in
difficult territory because the answer Beckett points to would seem
to lie beyond the theoretical and conceptual mode of knowledge
altogether and therefore beyond philosophy. This means that the
journey to the answer would involve philosophy only in the sense
that it would analyze philosophical thinking in order to find its way
out of it and to leave it behind.

To see what this might imply, let us consider again the philosophical problem we were discussing in the first chapter. There we
saw that the history of western philosophy from the pro-Socratics
to the present time has consisted largely of repeated attempts to fit
one metaphysical system or another on reality. The breakdown
of each of these systems under the critical scrutiny of other
philosophers, who ironically enough, and all the more damningly,
were often only trying to close the remaining loopholes in a system
they actually valued, has led over and over again to the *Angst* that
grows out of a combined sense of uprootedness, nostalgia, impo-
tence, and despair. Our own time feels this *Angst* with particular

intensity, and it is also perhaps the first period in history that instead of trying to flee from the discomfort of this into still another system is taking a critical look not only at the failed systems, but also at the very ideal of systematic understanding as such. This means that our present philosophical situation is both uniquely painful and perhaps potentially uniquely fruitful. That we are now calling system building itself into question places us in a position, for the first time, to become aware of the previously unconscious assumptions that have led us to seek system as a cognitive ideal because these have involved the supposition that being as such was a kind of system. The vision founded on these assumptions, I will refer to as essentialim.

What were these assumptions? The fundamental assumption, I think, is that being as such has the structure of formal logic. This is implicit in the Aristotelian ideal of knowledge as *"cognitio certa per causas"* : we know a thing truly when we know the network of causes to which it belongs, and when we know this, we can proceed by inference from the particular thing or event to the other components of the system. In the form in which this has developed in our tradition, it has been closely associated with the idea that the ontological structure of a particular entity has a fixed form, the essence, which determines all of the characteristics and activities of the entity according to an inner necessity; the essence is the guarantee of the predictability of the entity and consequently of the system of which it is a constituent part. One of the clearest forms this approach to metaphysics has taken can be seen in the thought of Leibniz, for whom every casual relation involved a necessary logical connection and who thought that an exhaustive knowledge of the essence of any entity would involve knowledge not only of what it now is but also of all of its future states until the end of time. This may seem extreme, but it is really only the carrying out to their logical conclusion of the essentialist assumptions. I would not wish to say that essentialism is the only possible form that the metaphysical enterprise can take — after all, the future may hold many surprises for us — but it has been so dominant in the metaphysical tradition of western philosophy until recently that many philosophers have assumed and still do assume that metaphysics and essentialism are identical.

It is significant that in attempting to define metaphysics, C. S. Peirce would say that "metaphysics consists in the results of the absolute acceptance of logical principles not merely as regulatively valid, but as truths of being."[5] In that statement Peirce made unusually clear the fundamental essentialist assumption, but the fact that he presented this as a definition not merely of one form of metaphysics, but of metaphysics as such, also shows how difficult it has been to conceive of an approach to the study of being that would not be essentialistically oriented.

In the last few centuries it has become increasingly difficult to continue trusting these assumptions, but for those in an earlier time who found it easier to trust them, they did offer many comforts, the loss of which has led to great discomfort on the part of the Roquentins and Vladimirs of modern literature. Essentialism did at least have the advantage of domesticating the universe of being, of mapping it out and labeling it conceptually so that once we had become acquainted with the map and learned some of the names on it, we were in a position to say, "Pot, pot," and be comforted. While we could do this, language was our home, not a prison, but this way of thinking and seeing is no longer as easy as it once was. For some, among whom Beckett and the more conscious of his characters would seem to be numbered, it has become impossible. I do not know how much Beckett has read of Ludwig Wittgenstein, but I think he would find congenial the description Wittgenstein gives us in the *Philosophical Investigations* of the way the conceptual forms embodied in language can impede a direct vision of reality : "A *picture* held us captive. And we could not get outside it, for it lay in our language and language seemed to repeat it to us inexorably."[6] And I suspect that Beckett would also feel a sympathy with the idea so frequently returned to by Wittgenstein that philosophy is a kind of therapy that seeks to bring about the conditions for silence and that finds its success not in the solution of a problem, but in the vanishing of the problem. So, similarly, when we study philosophy in the context of Beckett's novels and plays, it is only for the purpose of sweeping philosophy away.

To sweep philosophy away, however, is not something that can be carried out very easily, because this would require us to reject its comforts along with its frustrations. The philosophical *Angst* of the twentieth century is partially disappointment with the collapsed ideal of the essentialist enterprise, the homesickness of those who miss the good old days of the old questions and the old answers, the days when pots were pots, and it is partially also the frustrated rage of those who wish to break out of the net of concepts but because of the persistence of old habits find that with every step they become newly entangled. Often, in fact, both attitudes are present simultaneously, as in the case of Lucky in *Godot,* whose monologue is an aspect of the very trap he dramatizes his frustration with in the dance he calls "The Net." It is probably because Beckett depicts this anguish that he has acquired the reputation of a gloomy, despairing writer, but although Beckett does portray this, his vision is not limited to it; it reaches beyond this toward the direct seeing and interior silence that so many of his characters both long for and fear.

I think that seeing the philosophical concern of Beckett's works in this larger context and also seeing the ambiguity of response it evokes both in his works and in our culture as a whole can help us to understand more clearly what the transformation he is pointing to would consist in and why it would have both philosophical and moral aspects. It would be philosophical in that it would require careful thought in the service of clarity of mind, but since it would culminate not in a change in what is seen but in a new way of seeing, it would also require the breakup of all the habits that supported the old vision. The eyes that are rising from the depths of Winnie's being in *Happy Days,* the eyes that are seeking O in *Film,* and the eyes that would see the stars in *Cascando* are the true eyes of the characters represented, and therefore they cannot cease to pursue them, but they will not be able to open and see until the characters give up the illusions and habits of evasion that they have mistakenly identified their very lives with. The moral critique that the plays indirectly present is an analysis of the evasions that inhibit authentic vision. In fact, one might say that in all of Beckett's works, philosophy is simply an aspect of the psychology of the characters. The ego, with all of its habits of distorting reality or trying to impose itself on it, is one more screen, like the screen of concepts and ratiocination (which itself becomes one of the ego's mechanisms), that interposes itself between the true eyes and direct awareness of being. In the various plays we see these patterns of habit in different stages of dissolution or stalemate, depending on the case. Where there is a possibility that they could go on to finally dissolve and vanish, the interest of this for the play is that the characters in which it is taking place might through this process of inner death and liberation become at last themselves. For becoming themselves is the essential step to seeing with their own eyes, and this in turn is what alone can usher them into direct vision and silence, a peace that would, quite literally, pass understanding because it would be the very immediateness of their lives — their own hearts' truth, their own hearts' love, their own hearts' hate.

NOTES

CHAPTER I: INTRODUCTION

[1]Matthew Arnold, "Preface to First Edition of *Poems* (1853)," *On the Classical Tradition*, ed. R. H. Super (Ann Arbor: University of Michigan Press, 1960), pp. 2-3.

[2]Marjorie Hope Nicolson, *The Breaking of the Circle* (New York: Columbia University Press, 1960).

[3]Arnold, "Preface to First Edition," p. 1.

[4]The opening line of the *Metaphysics*, in *The Basic Works of Aristotle*, ed. Richard McKeon (New York: Random House, 1941), p. 689.

[5]Beckett studied French and Italian at Trinity College, Dublin (B.A., 1929; M.A., 1931), and at one time intended to take up an academic career. His master's thesis was on Descartes.

[6]See Ruby Cohn, "Philosophical Fragments in the Works of Samuel Beckett," in *Samuel Beckett: A Collection of Critical Essays*, ed. Martin Esslin (Englewood Cliffs, N.J.: Prentice Hall, 1965), pp. 169-77.

[7]Samuel Beckett, *Waiting for Godot* (New York: Grove Press, 1954), p. 41a. The play originally appeared in French as *En attendant Godot* (Paris: Éditions de Minuit, 1952) and was translated by the author himself. The Grove Press edition numbers only the left hand pages; to indicate that a quotation is from the right hand page, I will insert the letter "a" after the page number, as in this case. Subsequent page references will be given in parentheses.

[8]Aristotle, *De Anima*, in *Basic Works*, p. 553.

[9]Philip Wheelwright, ed. *The Presocratics* (New York: Odyssey Press, 1966), p. 70.

[10]Ibid, p. 71.

[11]Ibid, p. 74.

[12]Ibid, p. 79.

[13]Ibid, p. 72.

[14]Samuel Beckett, *Endgame* (New York: Grove Press, 1958), p. 70. The play originally appeared in French as *Fin de partie* (Paris: Éditions de Minuit, 1957) and was translated by the author. Subsequent page references refer to the Grove Press edition and are given in parentheses.

[15]All of the above passages from Democritus may be found on pages 182-83 of Wheelwright, *The Presocratics*.

[16]Samuel Beckett, *Murphy* (New York: Grove Press, 1957), pp. 3-4. See William York Tindall, *Samuel Beckett* (New York: Columbia University Press, 1964), p. 14.

[17]Samuel Beckett, *Watt* (New York: Grove Press, 1959), p. 34. See Tindall, *Samuel Beckett*, p. 20.

[18]*Murphy*, p. 47.

[19]Wheelwright, *The Presocratics*, p. 239.

[20]See Eugene Webb, *Samuel Beckett: A Study of His Novels* (Seattle: University of Washington Press, 1970; London: Peter Owen, 1970); pp. 22-25.

[21]In Samuel Beckett, *Poems in English* (New York: Grove Press, 1961), pp. 11-17. See Webb, *Beckett: Novels,* pp. 26-27.

[22]See Webb, *Beckett: Novels,* pp. 26-27, 44.

[23]Berkeley is mentioned in Lucky's speech in *Waiting for Godot,* p. 29, and the Berkeleian principle, *"esse est percipi,"* is cited by Beckett himself in the notes to *Film,* in Samuel Beckett, *Cascando and Other Dramatic Works* (New York: Grove Press, 1968), p. 75.

[24]*Purgatorio,* canto IV. Beckett named the protagonist of his early collection of stories, *More Pricks Than Kicks* (London: Chatto and Windus, 1934), after this figure. See Webb, *Beckett: Novels,* pp. 23, 44-45.

[25]See Webb, *Beckett: Novels,* pp. 24, 62-63.

[26]The volumes of the trilogy originally appeared as *Molloy* (Paris, 1951), *Malone meurt* (Paris, 1951), and *L'Innomable* (Paris, 1953), and were all published by Éditions de Minuit. The English translations, all published by Grove Press, are *Molloy* (New York, 1955), *Malone Dies* (New York, 1956), and *The Unnamable* (New York, 1958). All translations are by Samuel Beckett himself except in the case of *Molloy,* which he translated in collaboration with Patrick Bowles.

[27]David Hume, *A Treatise of Human Nature,* ed. L. A. Selby-Bigge (Oxford: Clarendon Press, 1888), p. 253.

[28]See Edwin Arthur Burtt, *The Metaphysical Foundations of Modern Physical Science* (London: Routledge and Kegan Paul, 1932), pp. 52-55, 63.

[29]The importance of atomism in our century is obvious. Hylozoism can be seen in recent attempts to trace all matter to a common origin in a single element, hydrogen for example, and in the close association between spirit and matter in a thinker like Teilhard de Chardin.

[30]*The Unnamable,* p. 70.

[31]A chronology of Beckett's works, giving both the dates of composition and the dates of publication (which sometimes differ considerably), may be found in Hugh Kenner, *Samuel Beckett: A Critical Study* (New York: Grove Press, 1961; Berkeley and Los Angeles: University of California Press, 1968), pp. 26-28.

[32]*Bram van Velde* (New York: Grove Press, 1960), p. 13.

[33]Ibid., p. 10.

[34]Ibid., pp. 10-13.

[35]Samuel Beckett as quoted in Tom F. Driver, "Beckett by the Madeleine," *Columbia University Forum,* IV, no. 3 (Spring, 1961), 23.

[36]Israel Shenker, "Moody Man of Letters," *New York Times,* CV, sec. 2 (May 6, 1956), 1.

[37]Driver, "Beckett by the Madeleine," p. 22.

CHAPTER II: *WAITING FOR GODOT*

[1]The French text (p. 60) had "Catulle" rather than Adam, and this was carried over into the British text. "Adam" would appear to have been an emendation aimed at emphasizing the idea of universality. In Hebrew the word means "mankind."

[2]In Russian. The name was made famous by St. Vladimir or Vladimir I, who consolidated the Russian state at Kiev and imposed the Christian religion on its people.

[3]*Pozzo* means "pool" in Italian and is often used to mean "cesspool."

[4]Brecht proposed to have Pozzo called "von Pozzo" to emphasize his socioeconomic significance; see Georg Hensel, *Samuel Beckett* (Velber bei Hanover: Freidrich Verlag, 1968), p. 16. See also Henry Hewes, "Mankind in

the Merdecluse," in *Casebook on Waiting for Godot,* ed. Ruby Cohn (New York: Grove Press, 1967), p. 67.

[5]Pozzo says he took Lucky as a "knook." What a knook is is not explained in the English translation, but in the French (p. 5) Pozzo goes on to say, *"Autrefois on avait des bouffons. Maintenant on a des knouks"* ("Once one had fools. Now one has knooks"). A knook, then, would seem to be an intellectual in the modern world occupying a position somewhat like that of the court jester in the medieval. In both cases the master expects entertainment, but sometimes gets more.

[6]*Malone Dies,* p. 11.

[7]Beckett discusses the deadening power of habit in detail in *Proust* (New York: Grove Press, 1957), pp. 7-8.

[8]*Watt,* p. 21. See Webb, *Beckett: Novels,* pp. 65-66.

[9]*Watt,* p. 227.

[10]For a further elaboration of this image in a later work see Beckett's novel, *How It Is* (New York: Grove Press, 1964).

[11]In the French original (p. 104) Vladimir did remember the name of the man, a M. Bonnely at Rousillon. Evidently Beckett decided while making the translation that some additional uncertainty would be of value.

[12]In the French version the names are not Macon and Cackon, but Vaucluse and Merdecluse. The pun, however, works the same way.

[13]*Unnamable,* pp. 143, 152.

CHAPTER III: *ALL THAT FALL*

[1]In Samuel Beckett, *Krapp's Last Tape and Other Dramatic Pieces* (New York: Grove Press, 1960). Page references are given in parentheses.

[2]Psalms, 145:14.

[3]Dan is referring to the fate of the sorcerers and diviners in the fourth chasm of Malebolge in *Inferno,* Canto XX.

[4]See Webb, *Beckett: Novels,* pp. 50-51.

CHAPTER IV: *ENDGAME*

[1]Colin Duckworth, in 'The Making of *Godot,*" *Casebook,* ed. Cohn, p. 89, reports that *Godot* was written between October 9, 1948, and January 29, 1949, as an interlude during the writing of *Malone meurt.*

[2]See Webb, *Beckett: Novels,* pp. 111-13, 125, 128-29, 150.

[3]Letter of June 21, 1956, in *The Village Voice Reader,* ed. Daniel Wolf and Edwin Fancher (Garden City, N.Y.: Doubleday, 1962), p. 183.

[4]Eva Metman, "Reflections on Samuel Beckett's Plays," in *Samuel Beckett,* ed. Esslin, p. 120.

[5]See Beckett, *Proust,* pp. 17-21, for a discusion of Proust's idea of involuntary memory.

[6]According to the *Commentaria* of Simplicius. See Wheelwright, ed. *The Presocratics,* pp. 111-12.

[7]*Unnamable,* p. 143.

[8]It is possible that "Mother Pegg" may be an allusion on the part of the author to something in his own life. Peggy Guggenheim, in her memoirs, tells of how she tried, and failed, to draw Beckett into an emotional relationship with her. See Marguerite Guggenheim, *Out of This Century* (New York: Dial Press, 1946), pp. 194ff.

[9]The translation of certain phrases in the French original as Shakespearean tags emphasizes Hamm's tendency to play the actor. *"Mon royaume pour un boueux"* (French, p. 38), for example, becomes "my king-

dom for a nightman" (English, p. 23); "nightman" as a play on the horse-like figure that represents the knight in chess makes this a pun on "my king-dom for a horse," the words of another ruined monarch in *King Richard III*. *"Finie la rigolade"* in the French text (p. 78) becomes Prospero's "my revels now are ended" (English, p. 56) from *The Tempest*.

[10]In the French original (pp. 103-5) the episode of the discovery of the boy is much more elaborate, with definite religious overtones alluding to both Christian and oriental traditions. When Hamm hears about the boy he says, *"La pierre levée"* ("the lifted stone"), and when he surmises, *"Il regarde la maison sans doute, avec les yeux de Moïse mourant"* ("No doubt he is looking at the house with the eyes of the dying Moses"), Clov answers that he is contemplating his navel. When translating the play Beckett must have decided that these allusions were too specific and distracting. Cf. Martin Esslin, *The Theatre of the Absurd* (New York: Doubleday, 1961), p. 35-37.

CHAPTER V: *KRAPP'S LAST TAPE*

[1]*Proust*, pp. 2-3.

[2]The text of the play appears in *Krapp's Last Tape and Other Dramatic Pieces*. Page references are given in parentheses. The play was first produced in 1958.

[3]*Proust*, p. 8.

[4]This also seems to have been the book Dan and Maddy Rooney were reading together in *All That Fall*, p. 70.

CHAPTER VI: *EMBERS*

[1]The text appears in *Krapp's Last Tape and Other Dramatic Pieces*. Page references are given in parentheses.

[2]It may have been for this reason that Beckett gave Henry a name that means "head of the family," from the German *Heimrih*. See Ruby Cohn, *Samuel Beckett: The Comic Gamut* (New Brunswick, N.J.: Rutgers University Press, 1962), p. 250.

[3]Canto III, lines 34-42.

CHAPTER VII: TWO MIMES

[1]Page references are not provided for either mime, since both are very short. *Act Without Words I* appears in both *Endgame* and *Krapp's Last Tape and Other Dramatic Pieces*. *Act Without Words II* appears in the latter only.

[2]Beckett mentioned Heidegger in the interview with Tom Driver, "Beckett by the Madeleine," p. 23. See also Webb, *Beckett: Novels*, p. 18. For Heidegger's discussion of his concept of *Geworfenheit* see Martin Heidegger, *Sein und Zeit* (Halle: Max Niemeyer, 1929), I, 135: English translation, *Being and Time*, trans. John Macquarrie and Edward Robinson (Oxford: Basil Blackwell, 1962), p. 174.

[3]New York: Harcourt Brace, 1925. See, for example, the photograph facing page 144 which shows a chimpanzee piling up boxes in order to climb up to a bunch of bananas.

[4]See Webb, *Beckett: Novels*, under "Compulsions, theme of" in index, p. 186.

CHAPTER VIII: *HAPPY DAYS*

[1]New York: Grove Press, 1961. Page references are given in parentheses.

[2]*Waiting for Godot*, p. 58a.

[3]I am indebted to Ruby Cohn for the identification of many of Winnie's quotations and allusions. For a more extensive study of this subject see Cohn, *Samuel Beckett,* pp. 253-59.

CHAPTER IX: *WORDS AND MUSIC*

[1]The text appears in Samuel Beckett, *Cascando and Other Short Dramatic Pieces* (New York: Grove Press, 1968). Page references are given in parentheses.

CHAPTER X: *CASCANDO*

[1]The text of *Cascando* appears in *Cascando and Other Short Dramatic Pieces.* Page references are given in parentheses.

CHAPTER XI: TRIOS

[1]The texts of both of these plays appear in *Cascando and Other Short Dramatic Pieces.* Page references for *Play* are given in parentheses, but since *Come and Go* is only three pages long, page references for that work will not be necessary.

[2]See Webb, *Beckett: Novels,* pp. 163-68. Marcel Mihalovici, who wrote the musical score for *Cascando* and who has written an operatic setting for *Krapp's Last Tape* (the opera is called *Krapp*), says that Beckett is "a remarkable musician" and was able to give him valuable help in the composition of the scores they worked on together. See Marcel Mihalovici, "My Collaboration with Samuel Beckett," in *Beckett at 60,* ed. John Calder (London: Calder and Boyars, 1967), pp. 20-21.

CHAPTER XII: *FILM*

[1]The text appears in *Cascando and Other Short Dramatic Pieces.* It has also been published separately as *Film* (New York: Grove Press, 1969), with an essay on directing *Film* by Alan Schneider. Page references to the *Cascando* edition will be given in parentheses. The film as produced is substantially but not entirely identical with the film described by the text. It was produced in 1964 by Evergreen Theatre, Inc., starring Buster Keaton and directed by Alan Schneider.

[2]George Berkeley, "A Treatise Concerning the Principles of Human Knowledge," in *Essay, Principles, Dialogues,* ed. Mary Whiton Calkins (New York: Scribner's, 1929), p. 126.

[3]The film as produced cut the opening scene and began, after titles superimposed on a shot of Keaton's eyes, with the episode of the elderly couple which begins on page 77 of *Cascando and Other Short Dramatic Pieces.* According to Alan Schneider the cut was not for aesthetic reasons but simply because the crowd scenes did not turn out well in the take and it would have been too expensive to do them again (see Schneider's essay in *Film,* p. 77).

[4]In the actual film he also has to deal with the eye-like effect of the eyelets of his folder before he can get to the pictures. The chair that was used turned out to have holes resembling eyes in its headrest, but these do not seem to bother him.

[5]If it is his mother's room, he is not the first of Beckett's characters to have journeyed on such a quest. Molloy had also travelled in search of his mother and began his narrative with the statement: "I am in my mother's room. It's I who live there now" (*Molloy,* p. 7).

⁶Except for the eyes, which are not visible, this is a perfect description of a photograph of Samuel Beckett himself kneeling as a child at his mother's knees. The photograph may be seen facing page 24 in *Beckett at 60*. The photograph used in the actual film is also of a child praying in the presence of his mother, but it is generally quite different from the description.

⁷In Beckett's works generally, hats are closely identified with the identities and ways of thinking of characters. See Webb, *Beckett: Novels*, pp. 70 and 95-96, for hats in the novels.

⁸See note 7 above. The hat used in the actual film was Keaton's own porkpie. See *Film*, p. 72.

CHAPTER XIII: *EH JOE*

¹The text appears in *Cascando and Other Short Dramatic Pieces*. Page references are given in parentheses.

CHAPTER XIV: A GENERAL VIEW

¹*Molloy*, p. 52.

²"*Nicht über Philosophie, sondern über Situationen*," (Hensel, *Beckett*, p. 43).

³"*Der dieses Spieles nicht*" (ibid., p. 44).

⁴See above, note 6, Chapter XII.

⁵*The Collected Papers of Charles Sanders Peirce*, ed. Charles Hartshorne and Paul Weiss (Cambridge, Mass.: Harvard University Press, 1960), Vol. I, par. 487.

⁶Trans. G. E. M. Anscombe (New York: Macmillan, 1953), par. 115.

LIST OF FIRST PERFORMANCES

This list is in chronological order by play and gives the dates, locations, and directors of first performances of both French and English versions. Where works received their initial productions in other languages this is indicated as well.

En attendant Godot: Paris, Théâtre de Babylone, directed by Roger Blin, January 5, 1953. *Waiting for Godot*: London, Arts Theatre Club, directed by Peter Hall, August 3, 1955.

All That Fall: London, BBC, directed by Donald McWhinnie, January 13, 1957. *Tous ceux qui tombent*: Paris, O.R.T.F., directed by Alain Trutat, December 19, 1959.

Fin de partie: London, Royal Court Theatre, directed by Roger Blin, April 3, 1957. *Endgame*: New York, Cherry Lane Theater, directed by Alan Schneider, January 28, 1958.

Act Without Words I: London, Royal Court Theatre, directed by and starring Deryk Mendel, April 3, 1957.

Krapp's Last Tape: London, Royal Court Theatre, directed by Donald McWhinnie, October 28, 1958. *La dernière bande:* Paris, Théâtre Récamier, directed by Roger Blin, March 22, 1960.

Embers: London, BBC, directed by Donald McWhinnie, June 24, 1959.

Act Without Words II: London, Institute of Contemporary Arts, directed by Michael Horovitz, January 25, 1960.

Happy Days: New York, Cherry Lane Theater, directed by Alan Schneider, September 17, 1961. *Oh, les beaux jours*: Paris, Odéon-Théâtre de France, directed by Roger Blin, October 29, 1963.

Words and Music (Music by John Beckett): London, BBC, directed by Michael Bakewell, November 13, 1962.

Play: First produced in German as *Spiel*: Ulm, Ulmer Theater, directed by Deryk Mendel, June 14, 1963. *Play*: New York, Cherry Lane Theater, directed by Alan Schneider, January 4, 1964. *Comédie*: Paris, Pavillon de Marsan, directed by Jeane-Marie Serreau, June 14, 1964.

Cascando: Paris, O.R.T.F., directed by Roger Blin, October 13, 1963. London: BBC, directed by Donald McWhinnie, October 6, 1964.

Film: directed by Alan Schneider and starring Buster Keaton, Venice Film Festival, September 4, 1965.

Come and Go: First produced in German as *Kommen und Gehen*: Berlin, Werkstatt des Schiller-Theaters, directed by Deryk Mendel, January 14, 1966. *Va et vient*: Paris, Odéon-Théâtre de France, directed by Samuel Beckett, February 28, 1966. *Come and Go*: Dublin, Peacock Theater, directed by Edward Golden, February 28, 1968.

Eh Joe: First produced in German as *He, Joe*: Süddeutscher Rundfunk,

149

directed by Samuel Beckett, April 13, 1966. *Eh Joe*: London, BBC, directed by Alan Gibson, July 4, 1966.

Breath: New York, Eden Theatre, June 16, 1969.

BIBLIOGRAPHY

This bibliography is in two sections. The first is a list in chronological order of the principal French, British, and American editions of Beckett's plays. The second section is a selective list of criticism limited to works that I think would be useful to a person interested in making a further study of Beckett's plays. I do not list separately articles in special issues or collections. There is a list of biographical sources and of criticism on the novels in the bibliography of my previous volume, *Samuel Beckett: A Study of His Novels* (Seattle: University of Washington Press, 1970; London: Peter Owen, 1970). To that list of biographical sources should now be added John Calder, ed., *Beckett at 60,* James Knowlson, ed., *Samuel Becket: An Exhibition,* and Alec Reid, *All I Can Manage, More than I Could,* all three included in the list below. For further bibliographical information the reader should see the critical bibliography, *Samuel Beckett: His Works and His Critics,* by Raymond Federman and John Fletcher (Berkeley and Los Angeles: University of California Press, 1970). For the most recent material there is, of course, the *PMLA* annual bibliography, in which Beckett is listed under French writers.

Principal Editions of Beckett's Plays in Chronological Order

En Attendant Godot. Paris: Éditions de Minuit, 1952. Scholarly edition annotated by Germaine Brée and Eric Schoenfeld, published in New York by Macmillan, 1963.

Waiting for Godot, trans. Samuel Beckett. New York: Grove Press, 1954. London: Faber and Faber, 1956. Translation of *En Attendant Godot.*

Fin de partie and *Acte sans paroles.* Published in one volume. Paris: Éditions de Minuit, 1957.

All That Fall. London: Faber and Faber, 1957. New York: Grove Press, 1957. Reprinted in *Krapp's Last Tape and Other Dramatic Pieces.* New York: Grove Press, 1960.

Tous ceux qui tombent, trans. Robert Pinget and Samuel Beckett. Paris: Éditions de Minuit, 1957. French translation of *All That Fall.*

Endgame and *Act without Words,* both translated by Samuel Beckett and published in one volume. New York: Grove Press, 1958. London: Faber and Faber, 1958. Translations of *Fin de partie* and *Actes sans paroles.*

Krapp's Last Tape, Evergreen Review, II, No. 5 (Summer, 1958), 13-24. Reprinted in *Krapp's Last Tape and Other Dramatic Pieces,* 1960.

Embers, Evergreen Review, III, No. 10 (November-December, 1959), 24-41. Reprinted in *Krapp's Last Tape and Other Dramatic Pieces,* 1960. Radio play.

151

La dernière bande and *Cendres*. Both published in one volume. *La dernière bande* was translated by Pierre Leyris and Samuel Beckett, *Cendres* by Robert Pinget and Samuel Beckett. Paris: Éditions de Minuit, 1959. Translations of *Krapp's Last Tape* and *Embers*.

Act without Words II, translated from the French by Samuel Beckett, *New Departures,* No. 1 (Summer, 1959), pp. 89-91. Reprinted in *Krapp's Last Tape and Other Dramatic Pieces,* 1960.

Happy Days. New York: Grove Press, 1961. London: Faber and Faber, 1962.

Words and Music, Evergreen Review, VI, No. 27 (November-December, 1962,) 34-43. Reprinted in *Cascando and Other Short Dramatic Pieces.* New York: Grove Press, 1968.

Cascando, Evergreen Review, VII, No. 30 (May-June, 1963), 47-57. Reprinted in *Cascando and Other Short Dramatic Pieces,* 1968.

Oh les beaux jours, trans. Samuel Beckett. Paris: Éditions de Minuit, 1963. Translation of *Happy Days.*

Play. London: Faber and Faber, 1964. Appears in *Cascando and Other Short Dramatic Pieces,* 1968.

Comédie, trans. Samuel Beckett. *Lettres Nouvelles,* XII (June-July-August, 1954), 10-31. Translation of *Play.*

Comédie et Actes divers. Paris: Éditions de Minuit, 1966. Collection of theatrical pieces: *Comédie, Va et vient, Cascando, Paroles et musique, Dis Joe, Actes sans paroles II.*

Come and Go: A Dramaticule. London: Calder and Boyars, 1967. Appears in *Cascando and Other Short Dramatic Pieces,* 1968.

Film: In *Cascando and Other Short Dramatic Pieces,* 1968. Published separately by Grove Press in 1969.

Eh Joe. In *Cascando and Other Short Dramatic Pieces,* 1968.

Selected Criticism

Alpaugh, David J. "Negative Definition in Samuel Beckett's *Happy Days.*" *Twentieth Century Literature,* XI (1966), 202-10.

Ashmore, Jerome. "Philosophical Aspects of *Godot.*" *Symposium,* XVI (1962), 296-306.

Bensky, Roger. "La symbolique du mime dans le théâtre de Beckett." *Lettres Nouvelles,* Sept.-Oct., 1969, pp. 157-63.

Brown, John Russel. "Mr. Beckett's Shakespeare." *Critical Quarterly,* V (1963), 310-26. On *Waiting for Godot.*

Calder, John, ed. *Beckett at 60: A Festschrift.* London: Calder and Boyars, 1967.

Chevigny, Bell G., ed. *Twentieth Century Interpretations of* Endgame. Englewood Cliffs, N.J.: Prentice Hall, 1969.

Cohen, Robert S. "Parallels and the Possibility of Influence between Simone Weil's *Waiting for God* and Samuel Beckett's *Waiting for Godot.*"

Modern Drama, VI (1964), 425-36.

Cohn, Ruby. *Samuel Beckett: The Comic Gamut.* New Brunswick, N.J.: Rutgers University Press, 1962.

——, ed. *Modern Drama,* IX (Dec., 1966), 237-346. Special issue on Beckett.

——, ed. *Casebook on Waiting for Godot.* New York: Grove Press, 1967.

Curnow, D. H. "Language and Theatre in Beckett's 'English' Plays." *Mosaic,* II, no. 1 (1968), 54-65.

Davie, Donald. "Kinds of Comedy." *Spectrum,* II (Winter, 1958), 25-31. On *All That Fall.*

Dukore, Bernard F. "The Other Pair in *Waiting for Godot.*" *Drama Survey* VII (1969), 133-37.

Driver, Tom F. "Beckett by the Madeleine." *Columbia University Forum,* IV, no. 3 (Spring, 1961), 21-25.

Easthope, Anthony. "Hamm, Clov, and Dramatic Method in *Endgame.*" *Modern Drama,* X (1968), 424-33.

Eastman, Richard M. "Samuel Beckett and *Happy Days.*" *Modern Drama,* VI (1964), 417-24.

Esprit, CCCXXXVIII (May, 1965), 801-1040. Special issue on modern theatre.

Esslin, Martin. *The Theatre of the Absurd.* New York: Doubleday, 1961.

——, ed. *Samuel Beckett: A Collection of Critical Essays.* Englewood Cliffs, N.J.: Prentice Hall, 1965.

Federman, Raymond. "Film." *Film Quarterly,* XX (Winter, 1966-67), 46-51.

Findlay, Robert R. "Confrontation in Waiting: *Godot* and the Wakefield Play." *Renascence,* XXI (1969), 195-202.

Fischer, Ernst. "Samuel Beckett: *Play* and *Film.*" *Mosaic,* II, no. 2 (1969), 96-116.

Fletcher, John. "The Arrival of Godot." *Modern Language Review,* LXIV (1969), 34-48.

——, "Balzac and Beckett Revisited." *French Review,* XXXVII (Oct., 1963), 78-80. On *Waiting for Godot.*

——, *Samuel Beckett's Art.* London: Chatto and Windus, 1967; New York: Barnes and Noble, 1967.

Frisch, Jack E. "*Endgame:* A Play as Poem." *Drama Survey,* III (1963), 257-63.

Gilbert, Sandra M. " 'All the Dead Voices': A Study of *Krapp's Last Tape.*" *Drama Survey,* VI (1968), 244-57.

Guicharnaud, Jacques, with June Guicharnaud. *Modern French Theater from Giraudoux to Genet.* Revised edition. New Haven, Conn.: Yale University Press, 1967.

Hensel, Georg. *Samuel Beckett.* Velber bei Hannover: Friedrich Verlag, 1968.

Jacobsen, Josephine, and William R. Mueller. *The Testament of Samuel Beckett*. New York: Hill and Wang, 1964.

Janvier, Ludovic. "Les difficultés d'un séjour." *Critique*, XXV (1969), 312-23.

Kenner, Hugh. *Samuel Beckett: A Critical Study*. New York: Grove Press, 1961; London: John Calder, 1962. New revised edition, Berkeley and Los Angeles: University of California Press, 1968.

Kern, Edith. "Beckett's Knight of Infinite Resignation." *Yale French Studies*, XXIX (Spring-Summer, 1962), 49-56. On *Happy Days*.

———. "Drama Stripped for Inaction: Beckett's *Godot*." *Yale French Studies*, XIV (Winter, 1954-55), 41-47.

Knowlson, James, ed. *Samuel Beckett: An Exhibition*. Foreword by A. J. Leventhal. London: Turret Books, 1971.

Kolve, V. A. "Religious Language in *Waiting for Godot*." *Centennial Review*, XI (1967), 102-27.

Mayoux, Jean-Jacques. "Samuel Beckett, homme de théâtre." *Livres de France*, XVIII (Jan., 1967), 14-21.

———. "Le théâtre de Samuel Beckett." *Études Anglaises*, X (1957), 350-66.

Mazars, Pierre, and Marcel Lasseaux. "A propos de *Comédie*." *Livres de France*, XVIII (Jan., 1967), 22.

Mélèse, Pierre. *Samuel Beckett*. Paris: Pierre Seghers, 1966.

Murch, Anne C. "Les indications scéniques dans le Nouveau Théâtre: *Fin de Partie*, de Samuel Beckett." *Australian Journal of French Studies*, VI (1969), 55-64.

O'Nan, Martha. *Samuel Beckett's Lucky: Damned*. Athens: Ohio University Modern Language Department, 1965. Nine-page pamphlet.

Oster, Rose-Marie G. "Hamm and Hummel: Beckett and Strindberg on the Human Condition.' *Scandinavian Studies*, XLI (1969), 330-45.

Reid, Alec. *All I Can Manage, More Than I Could: An Approach to the Plays of Samuel Beckett*. Dublin: The Dolmen Press, 1968.

Robinson, Michael. *The Long Sonata of the Dead*. London: Rupert Hart-Davis, 1969.

Schneider, Alan. "On Directing *Film*." In Samuel Beckett, *Film*. New York: Grove Press, 1969. Pp. 63-94.

———, "Reality Is Not Enough." *Tulane Drama Review*. IX (1965), 118-52.

———, "Waiting for Beckett: A Personal Chronicle." *Chelsea Review*, II (Autumn, 1958), 3-20.

Schoell, Konrad. "The Chain and the Circle: A Structural Comparison of *Waiting for Godot* and *Endgame*." *Modern Drama*, XI (1968), 48-53.

———,*Das Theater Samuel Becketts*. (Freiburger Schriften zur romanischen Philologie 11.) Munich: Wilhelm Fink, 1967.

Shenker, Israel. "Moody Man of Letters." The New York *Times*, CV, sec. 2 (May 6, 1956), 1.

Taylor, Andrew. "The Minimal Affirmation of *Godot.*" *Critical Review,* XII (1969), 3-14.

Todd, Robert E. "Proust and Redemption in *Waiting for Godot.*" *Modern Drama,* X (1967), 175-81.

Torrance, Robert M. "Modes of Being and Time in the World of *Godot.*" *Modern Language Quarterly,* XXVIII (1967), 77-95.

Trousdale, Marion. "Dramatic Form: The Example of *Godot.*" *Modern Drama,* XI (1968), 1-9.

Weales, Gerald. "The Language of *Endgame.*" *Tulane Drama Review,* VI (June, 1962), 107-17.

INDEX